Adult Education Procedures

Adult Education
PROCEDURES

A Handbook of Tested Patterns
for Effective Participation

PAUL BERGEVIN

DWIGHT MORRIS

ROBERT M. SMITH

THE SEABURY PRESS · NEW YORK

404-972-C-20-3.5
Fifth Printing

© 1963 by The Seabury Press, Incorporated
Library of Congress Catalog Card Number: 62-15233
ISBN:0-8164-2000-9
Printed in the United States of America

First *Seabury Paperback* edition printed in 1966.

PREFACE

This book is designed as a handbook for those persons who select and use procedures for adult education in the great number and variety of institutions which make up the fabric of a free society. The authors are engaged in studying and teaching professionally in the field of adult education. The procedures described here have been developed and tested with many thousands of persons in hundreds of settings and situations. Every effort has been made to present this material in a simple, direct form, for use by large numbers of adults of varying educational background.

The authors deeply appreciate the assistance given by Professor Helen Duncan and Mrs. Marilyn Coia.

We dedicate this book to the idea that adults must continue to extend their horizons through education if free people are to survive.

P. B.
D. M.
R. M. S.

CONTENTS

Adult Education Procedures

CHAPTER 1

Introduction: Keeping Adult Education Procedures in Perspective

All over the world, people are undertaking lifelong education. Tens of millions are involved in learning activities in industry, schools, churches, clubs, and the armed forces. Almost all contemporary institutions and agencies make use of in-service education for their personnel. Workshops and institutes are held for thousands of groups for countless different purposes. Despite their varied purposes, these activities have one thing in common: the adult education procedures involved in planning and conducting them.

Every meeting has had some planning, and makes use of some procedure to facilitate learning (for example, a speech or group discussion); but often the learning activities are not as productive as they might be if the participants had a better working knowledge of tested, useful procedures and of what happens when these procedures are used in adult education activities. This handbook is designed principally to assist in the selection and use of procedures. It contains descriptions of

(1) a tested six-step procedure for planning adult education activities (Chapter 2).

(2) fourteen effective *techniques* for arranging relationships among adults in learning situations—for example, the panel, group discussion, and the demonstration (Chapter 3).

(3) six useful *subtechniques* for supplementing a technique to meet the requirements of a particular learning situation—for example, buzz sessions and the question period (Chapter 4).

(4) five commonly used resources to aid learning (educational aids)—for example, the exhibit and the case history (Chapter 5). In addition there are suggestions for designing clinics, institutes, and workshops (Chapter 6), a list of suggested readings, and a glossary of useful terms.

I. Some Key Terms

These are the key terms used in this book: *technique, subtechnique,* and *educational aid.* The reader will find these terms in the glossary, and he will also find them explained at the beginning of the respective chapters devoted to these three procedures. Another term needs clarification here. We have been using the words *adult education* to refer to any learning situation or activity involving physically-mature people. For purposes of discussing procedures, however, it is necessary to have a narrower definition of adult education—one that permits us to distinguish adult education from (for example) recreation or from the random learning that takes place when we watch a television program.

In this book we will be using adult education to refer to the process through which adults have and use opportunities to learn *systematically under the guidance of an agent, a teacher, or a leader.* This process can be regarded as a continuing cycle of planning, conducting, and evaluating of learning activities for adults. It is a process that requires guidance by a trained teacher or leader who can assist the learner to strive for desirable goals related to ideals and values that he believes to be worth attaining. Random learning may take place at any moment in the adult's experience; but it is purposeful, guided learning that we are concerned with here.

II. The Limitations of Procedures

Whenever we use adult education procedures, we should remember that each group is unique and that each person in the group is unique. A procedure which is appropriate for one group might be ill-suited to another group. A procedure that works well one week may get different results a week later with the same group. Careful diagnosis of the situation usually reveals that there were differences in the composition and purpose of the group, or perhaps in the mood of the persons present. To use adult educational procedures effectively we must be sensitive to the fact that we are working with people—complex persons of flesh and blood—not statistical units or even mere members of a group. All the procedures ever devised will be of little value if we lack sound insights into human nature—*our own as well as the other person's.*

4

Those of us who have accepted the responsibility of assisting adults with their educational problems must be able to relate ourselves to them, their educational needs, and those human forces that motivate all of us.

Procedures are important. Their proper selection and use can mean the difference between ineffective adult education and that kind of adult education which

—actively involves the learner in the educational process;
—stimulates the learner to seek more knowledge;
—achieves the specific goals for which it is designed.

However, procedures are not panaceas. They are not magic pills that guarantee success. Group discussion is a case in point. Lately, there has been a tendency to move away from the exclusive use of the speech or lecture to some kind of group discussion. Unfortunately many of the participants, both leaders and members of groups, are untrained in the use of this or any other technique. In many cases, time has been wasted in talk with little purpose or direction and no discipline. As group discussion became more popular, it was sometimes used as the cure-all for adult learning ills. No one procedure suits all adult learning situations any more than aspirin cures all physical ailments.

We have all encountered the enthusiast who returns from a workshop, singing the praises of buzz groups, role-playing, or some other procedure. He sees his newly discovered pet as the answer to problems involving adult education procedure. But he soon sees that adult education is a complex process—far too demanding to permit a knowledge of one or two procedures to equip him for successful practice. Even a thorough knowledge of all the procedures described in this book will not guarantee success.

We must remind ourselves then, that the process (the way we carry on a program—the procedures used and what happens when they are used) is of little value if we have nothing to study —content (subject matter and what is said about it). It would be a waste of time to discuss this if it were not for the fact that some of us become so enamoured of the way a thing is done (process) that we begin to slight what it is that we are doing (content). We can become so concerned with the vehicle that we lose sight of where it is taking us. We see then that there are two

5

arms to an adult learning program: the *content* (what we are going to read, reflect, and talk about) and the *process* (how we do it and what happens to us while it's being done). Both of these factors are of vital concern for an effective program of adult learning.

III. SOME SUGGESTIONS

When we use procedures and become increasingly aware of "process," we also should keep in mind our ultimate goals. What do we hope to accomplish through adult education? An educational experience should do something to enlighten, to change, to elevate persons. We don't teach a subject for its own sake or lead a group in order to teach a subject. We teach and help people. Education involves changing human behavior. Toward what kind of behavior are we striving? How can we devise teaching-learning situations which will help us to become the kind of people we hope we might be? This is the task that confronts us.

IV. TRAINED LEADERSHIP IS NOT ENOUGH

This book rests on one other assumption—that all persons participating in adult education need to learn something about their responsibilities as learners. They need to *learn how to learn* in a cooperative and mutually supporting manner. Experience and research have shown that adults can be taught to identify needs, to plan and conduct their own learning activities. They can learn to discuss issues in a productive way, to deal with conflict in the learning situation and share in the evaluation of their learning experiences. This we call active participation in the learning situation.

Active participation takes place when a participant actively assumes one of these roles: leader, resource person, or group participant. These three roles define the different ways of participating. Leadership may be centered in the trainer or teacher at certain times. At other times it may be shared by the trainer, or teacher and learners. Serving as leader is one way to participate. The best leadership is that which is appropriate to the learning situation.

In the learning activity the group participant role is occupied at a given time by all participants who are not taking part as the

6

nominal leader or resource person. When the group participant accepts his role in a responsible way, he is sharing in the leadership. Even though he is not the nominal leader, when he participates responsibly he does so in ways that actively promote understanding and growth among all co-learners.

The role of resource person is occupied when a participant (trainer or group participant) serves the other participants by offering authoritative information and opinions gained from training and experience. When one accepts this idea—of training all participants in adult education process and procedure—he will come to regard adult education activities as opportunities for all persons involved in the learning venture constantly to improve their performance together—to become what can be called a learning team.

In short, adult education processes and procedures are means to achieve ends. They can be used for narrow, misguided purposes like

- —"putting over" an idea or a point of view;
- —meeting the needs of one person or the few at the expense of the many;
- —keeping people needlessly dependent and passive.

Or they can be used

- —to release our creative energies;
- —to assist adults gradually (with discipline) to assume responsibility for their own education;
- —to promote more mature behavior;
- —to teach us how to work and live together.

When these latter purposes are served, we are furthering the democratic process to which we so often pay lip service.

CHAPTER 2

Planning Adult Education Activities

I. The Need for Systematic Planning

Adult education is needed to help us to change—to acquire new
knowledge and understandings in order to help us to mature.
Careful planning can set the conditions for change. It is difficult
to name a more demanding task. Yet much of the planning by
adult education agencies is haphazard. Often the planning is the
last-minute, stop-gap kind of effort summed up in the phrase
"Whom can we get to talk to our group at the next meeting?"

If we are to take the task of planning our adult education
activities seriously, we will need a systematic approach. This
chapter (a) sets forth a tested procedure for planning, (b) describes a group in action using this planning procedure, and
(c) discusses this example in terms of the critical factors involved
in designing adult education activities.

II. Why Planning Is Important

A. *People are important*

When we plan haphazardly we imply that it matters little whether
or not adults spend their time profitably in the learning activity.
The activities we plan may command the minds, feelings, and
energies of a number of impressionable personalities for several
hours. Only if people are not important does it become unimpor-
tant to make every moment as effective as possible.

B. *Learning is the goal*

Often we lose sight of the fact that our workshops, courses, and
discussion groups are conducted to promote learning. Learning
presumes change. The learner becomes different than he was be-

8

fore the learning experience. Often we lose sight of the goal of assisting people to change—to become more mature than they are now. With this ultimate goal in mind, we will consider carefully how best to achieve the changes in behavior that seem most desirable.

C. Planning helps learning

Carrying out the planning process can be a valuable learning experience. Careful planning involves seeking information, considering alternatives, and making decisions. Through this process we can learn a great deal about resources, techniques, and the topic under consideration. Time spent in planning can be regarded as a rewarding experience.

III. Who Plans?

A. The leader or teacher plans

Sometimes adult education activities are planned primarily by one person. This kind of planning is most likely to occur when the person doing the planning knows a great deal about whatever is to be taught, while those for whom he is planning have little or no knowledge of the subject. For example, a teacher might plan a course in citizenship for a group of immigrants; or an employer might plan some learning activities to introduce new employees to his business and his business methods. A group of medical investigators who have discovered a new way of treating a disease might plan an institute to teach others how to carry out the new treatment.

B. The entire group plans

Sometimes it is practical and effective for an entire group to plan its learning activities. The group should not be too large. Its members should know how to plan, and they must be able to plan in an efficient and productive manner. Many small learning groups set aside a part of each meeting to plan future meetings. When properly carried out, this kind of planning can involve each person to the extent that he accepts active responsibility for the learning venture.

C. A committee plans

Because it is often impractical for an entire group to assume primary responsibility for planning, committees plan many adult learning activities. Even when one person is primarily responsible for planning, he often uses a committee to help him identify needs and interests of the learners.

A committee is most able to plan effectively if (1) it has a capable chairman, (2) its members know how to plan, (3) its responsibilities are clearly understood by all members, and (4) its membership is representative of the group as a whole.

A committee is representative if its members possess backgrounds, interests, and points of view that are approximately typical of the group as a whole. Suppose it were desirable for a committee to plan some in-service training activities for the staff of a hospital. In order to be truly representative of the hospital, the committee must contain at least one person from each of these groups: administration, nursing services, dietetics, pharmacology, records and admissions, laboratory, radiology, housekeeping, ambulance, and physicians.

IV. A FLEXIBLE PROCEDURE FOR PLANNING

The following approach reduces the complex task of planning adult learning activities to six specific steps. This procedure has been developed through research and tested with hundreds of groups.

This six-step procedure should be used flexibly—as a guide or framework upon which to build. It has proven to be equally useful for planning one meeting or a series, an entire course or a single session. It is designed to be used by a committee. This overview of the six-step procedure will be followed by an example of its use and a detailed discussion of each step.

Step 1. *Identify a common interest or need of those who will participate.* An interest is something the participants would like to learn about or come to understand better. We hear people say, "I am interested in world affairs." An interest can serve as a starting point in planning adult education activities. If given the opportunity, adults can usually identify something they would like to learn about. A need is a lack or a deficiency that may be

10

satisfied by means of a learning experience. Needs and interests are inter-related. Interests often point toward needs. In order to encourage participation, it is helpful to begin with a need or interest that is recognized as important by the learner.

Step 2. *Develop topics.* Topics are the specific problems, issues, questions, and concepts with which the learning activity will be concerned. Topics are developed by "breaking down" an interest or a need—usually into questions the group seeks to answer. This is the statement of the *content* of the meetings being planned. Once the planning committee has listed some topics, it refines them, restating whenever necessary, and eliminating duplications. Each meeting or session will treat several topics.

Step 3. *Set goals for the learning activity.* The planning committee sets goals in order to clarify what it hopes to accomplish. Goals are the objectives or ends toward which the learning activities are directed. Goals are always based on a system of values. Thus goals provide a basis for future evaluation. Goals also help the committee in establishing the learning activity into logical sequences, in selecting the resources and techniques to use, and in determining which topics to include or emphasize.

Step 4. *Select appropriate resources.* Resources are people and educational materials and aids from which the learners can seek information. Resources are used to furnish information about the topics and help the learners achieve their educational goals. Some resources are: people, films, filmstrips, slides, pictures, exhibits, case histories, annotated reading lists, information briefs, charts, maps, books, pamphlets, etc. (The educational aids described in Chapter 5 are resources.) The members of the learning group should also be regarded as resources since each has experience and knowledge that can be used in the learning situation.

Step 5. *Select appropriate educational techniques and sub-techniques.* A technique is a way of arranging the relationships of learners and resources to assist the learners to acquire knowledge in a learning situation. Examples are the speech, the panel, the colloquy, the field trip, and the demonstration. A subtechnique is an educational instrument employed to enhance the effective use of a technique. Examples are: buzz sessions, audience reaction teams, listening and observing groups, question periods, and screening panels. In addition to the information that has emerged during Steps 1 to 5 in the planning procedure, the planning committee bases its choice of techniques on the (1) size of the learning group, (2) characteristics of the group, (3) nature of the physical facilities to be used, and (4) the kind and quality of leadership available.

Step 6. *Outline each session and the various responsibilities to be carried out.* Each session or meeting should be outlined in detail and placed in a time schedule. Responsibilities should be assigned for such tasks as publicity; evaluation; preparing a printed program; obtaining and instructing leaders, moderators, chairmen, and resource persons. If the learning activity or series is to be given a theme, it is at this point that the theme is selected.

V. How To Use the Six-step Planning Procedure—An Example

The following example is designed to illustrate the six-step planning procedure in action.

A. *The situation*

The Lincoln Elementary School Parent-Teachers Association meets on the first Friday evening of each month during the school year. The school has eight grades, a principal, eight teachers, and 300 students. It is located in a middle-class suburban area in a medium-sized town.

The Parent-Teachers Association has 100 members, about 50 of whom regularly attend the meetings. The typical meeting takes the following form:

7:30-8:15 p.m. Old and new business (awards, committee reports, minutes, etc.)

8:15-8:45 p.m. Program (usually a speaker or a performance by some of the children)

8:45-9:00 p.m. Refreshments

The programs, which are hurriedly planned by a committee early each fall, are usually not effective as learning experiences and tend to have the following weaknesses:

1. They are not based on the felt or expressed needs and interests of the members;

2. No specific educational goals are set;

3. A wide variety of appropriate resources are not used;

4. The speech serves almost exclusively as the learning technique;

5. No systematic evaluation is undertaken;

6. The group fails to probe deeply into the topics it considers;

7. There is seldom any use of advance or follow-up study.

However, the parents and school personnel are sincere and willing to learn how to work together more effectively for better education for the youngsters.

One of the P.T.A. members, Dr. Jones (a physician), has recently had training in the six-step planning procedure. Dr. Jones is a member of the planning committee for the year's program.

At the November meeting, during the discussion of new business, a parent criticizes the school's handling of a disciplinary problem involving his child. A confusing and somewhat heated debate follows during which it becomes clear that there is a need for better understanding of discipline and of school policies and practices pertaining to discipline.

Someone then suggests that a committee plan a special meeting to study the problems arising out of the discipline misunderstanding. As there seems to be consensus on this suggestion, the president asks for volunteers to serve on this committee. In addition to Dr. Jones, two parents and two teachers volunteer. The principal agrees to be available to the committee for consultation. Dr. Jones is made chairman of the committee because of his recent training in program planning. The committee is representative of the total group since it includes men and women, teachers and parents, a professional man, a factory worker, and a housewife, a young teacher and an older one. In addition it has a member of the regular program committee.

PREPARING TO PLAN

When Dr. Jones convenes the planning committee at his home late in November, he has available a large easel with paper, a crayon, and masking tape with which to fasten sheets of paper to the wall of his recreation room. The room is well-lighted and free from noise or distraction.

13

Dr. Jones makes sure that the committee members know each other before beginning the task assigned to them. (The committee members have studied a brief mimeographed overview of the six-step procedure before coming to the meeting.) Next he briefly reviews the six-step procedure and discusses the responsibilities of the committee as he understands them:

1. To plan some special learning activities (for all interested parents and teachers) to treat the subject of "Discipline";
2. To relate these activities as effectively as possible to the regularly-scheduled meetings and programs of the Parent-Teacher Association.

He has found out that the P.T.A.'s regular meeting room will be available for use on all week-day evenings in January and February except Mondays and Fridays. He has secured the approval of the executive committee to spend up to $15 for the learning activities.

B. Planning with the six-step procedure

The committee works through the six-step procedure under the guidance of Dr. Jones. It takes them three two-hour meetings to complete the planning. (This time can be cut in half after a committee has familiarized itself with the procedure and learned to work as a team.)

Step 1. *Identifying a common need or interest.* All committee members were present at the recent P.T.A. meeting and heard the discussion about various problems relating to discipline. At first, there appears to them to be no problem with regard to Step 1 in the planning process. The P.T.A. seems to have presented the committee with a clear-cut need upon which to base its planning. However, the chairman writes the word "discipline" on the easel and encourages the committee members to discuss the term. As they discuss, it becomes clear that each person is approaching the problem from a slightly different point of view. When the chairman asks the group to state exactly what need they are setting out to satisfy, they find it difficult to agree on a precise statement. Is the need for the P.T.A. members:

14

a. To understand discipline as a term?
b. To agree on what constitutes good discipline?
c. To learn to work together in the interests of good discipline?

The discussion reflects these points of view as well as others. When the group seems to "bog down," Dr. Jones suggests that they temporarily suspend their efforts to state the need precisely and proceed to the next step in the planning procedure with the need stated as follows: "To learn more about discipline as it relates to home and school." The committee members accept this suggestion.

Step 2. *Developing topics.* The chairman assists the committee to list the questions, problems, issues, and concerns that come to mind with regard to the need the committee is setting out to satisfy. In other words, he asks, "What do we wish to learn?" He warns the committee against excessive discussion of each suggestion and the danger of beginning to answer the questions in the committee meeting rather than at the learning activity they are planning. The following topics are written on the easel and then revised and grouped.

TOPICS AS FIRST LISTED

1. What is discipline?
2. How are children disciplined?
3. Is whipping desirable?
4. Is punishment a good form of discipline?
5. What methods of discipline are used at our schools?
6. What are current trends in thinking about discipline in elementary schools?
7. What is the parent's responsibility?
8. How far do the teachers' prerogatives go?
9. What is the principal's role?
10. In what respects do home and school work at cross-purposes?
11. How can we promote home-school cooperation with regard to discipline?

After the topics have been listed they are revised, combined, and grouped in the following manner:

TOPICS REVISED AND GROUPED

The Meaning of Discipline:

1. What is discipline?
2. How are children disciplined?
3. Punishment and discipline
   a. Is punishment good discipline?
   b. Is severe punishment justifiable?
4. How is discipline taught?
5. What are current professional trends about discipline?

Discipline in Our School:

1. What point of view is held by the principal and teachers?
2. Are school personnel in general agreement?
3. What about punishment?
   a. How severe?
   b. How administered?
4. What are the responsibilities of the teachers, principal, and parents?

School-Home Relationships and Discipline:

1. Are school and home working at cross-purposes? If so, how?
2. What are the areas for better cooperation?
3. What steps can we take first?

Step 3. *Setting goals.* The committee then moves on to setting goals. Dr. Jones, the Chairman, asks "Why are we going to conduct these learning activities?" What do we hope to accomplish? The committee first identifies several possible goals and then reworks them and decides to select four goals on which to concentrate. After the goals have been revised, they are as follows:

1. To encourage parents and school personnel to clarify points of view about discipline;
2. To promote home-school cooperation regarding discipline;
3. To encourage parents and school personnel to better understand themselves as they relate to each other and to children;
4. To identify opportunities for additional study and action concerning home and school cooperation.

Step 4. *Selecting appropriate resources.* The committee concludes its first meeting at this point. The chairman asks one member to bring to the next meeting a list of resource people who might be used. He asks another to investigate what pamphlets and free materials are available. Another committee member agrees to search for films, filmstrips, and slides that relate directly to the topics and goals.

At its next meeting the committee discusses the available resources and agrees that the most appropriate ones for its purposes are:

1. A free 20-page pamphlet "Discipline and the Elementary School Child";
2. A 20-minute film entitled "Discipline in our Schools";
3. A professor of education at a nearby college.

It is also pointed out that the teachers and the principal as well as the parents themselves have experience and knowledge that can be useful in the learning activities being planned.

The committee then evaluates the resources. It is decided to obtain the free pamphlet in sufficient quantity to provide one for each home represented at the forthcoming learning activities. The film is rejected when its description in the catalogue reveals it to be inappropriate and out of date. There is agreement that the professor of education could work well with the group to be involved and has knowledge that the group will need. A committee member agrees to ask the professor of education if he will be willing to serve at one or more meetings of the group, what his fee will be, and what dates he will be available.

AN IMPORTANT DECISION

At this point the committee feels the need to decide more specifically the nature and extent of the activities to be conducted. It decides to hold three two-hour meetings on successive Wednesday nights in January (if the resource person is available to serve). This decision is made because (1) the topics fall into three related groups, each of which apparently can be adequately treated in one session; (2) six hours seems to be an appropriate amount of time considering the nature of the group, the resources available, and the goals.

Note: The committee then examines the types of meetings described in Chapter 6 and decides that the term "institute" best fits the series of learning activities it is planning. From this point, the committee refers to the learning experience it is planning as an *Institute.*

Step 5. *Selecting appropriate techniques and subtechniques.* Before taking this step in the planning procedure, the chairman assists the group to review the techniques and subtechniques available to it. He allows time for the committee to look over Chapters 3 and 4 of this book. Then he reviews the progress made thus far—the need, the topics, the goals, and the best available resources. The committee learns that the professor of education (whom we shall call Prof. Taylor) will be available for all three meetings. The task now is to select appropriate techniques for three two-hour meetings to be held on successive Wednesday nights. The committee lists several techniques which seem most appropriate for each meeting.

1ST MEETING

THE MEANING OF DISCIPLINE

Topics	*Most Likely Techniques*
1. What is discipline?	1. Speech (by Prof. Taylor)
2. How are children disciplined?	2. Interview (of Prof. Taylor)
3. Punishment and discipline a. Is punishment good discipline? b. Is severe punishment justifiable?	3. Colloquy (Prof. Taylor serves as resource person; parents and teachers used as audience representatives)
4. How is discipline taught?	
5. What are current professional trends in thinking about discipline?	

Principal Resources	*Goal*
1. Prof. Taylor 2. Pamphlet	To encourage parents and teachers to clarify their thinking about discipline.

Since the topics to be considered at the first meeting are largely requests for information, the techniques that seem most appropriate are those which allow an authority to present information. With only one such person available, the choice was soon narrowed to the use of the speech, the interview, or the colloquy. The committee finally selected the colloquy because:

1. The audience can become active participants after the audience representatives and the resource person have brought out essential information;

2. The use of audience representatives will promote teamwork among the participants;

3. The available resource person is known to be able to operate in a flexible manner.

2ND MEETING

DISCIPLINE IN OUR SCHOOL

Topics	*Most Likely Techniques*
1. The ideas and opinions of our principal and teachers.	1. Symposium (speeches by three teachers and principal).
2. Are school personnel in agreement?	2. Panel (discussion by the principal and three teachers).
3. What about punishment? a. How administered? b. How severe?	3. Panel-forum (panel discussion followed by discussion by entire group).
4. What are the responsibilities of the teacher, principal, and parent?	

Principal Resources	*Goals*
1. School principal	1. To encourage parents and teachers to clarify their points of view about discipline.
2. Teachers	
3. Prof. Taylor	2. To promote home-school cooperation in understanding discipline.

Since the topics seem to call for both the presentation of information (numbers 1 and 3) and discussion (numbers 2 and 4), the committee decides to have a panel-forum. Reasons for this choice are:

1. The teachers and principal prefer some kind of discussion;
2. The audience should be able to participate more intelligently in the forum after hearing the information and discussion by the panel members;
3. The physical arrangement is suitable for discussion by the entire audience (chairs can be arranged in a large semicircle during the forum);
4. Prof. Taylor is a well-qualified moderator for the panel-forum.

It is decided to modify the panel by means of listening groups (see p. 196). The audience will be divided into two groups—parents and school personnel. Each group will be given special instructions for listening to the panel discussion. Modifying the panel with this subtechnique should:

1. Promote active listening;
2. Set the stage for verbal participation during the forum.

3RD MEETING

SCHOOL-HOME RELATIONS TO THE DISCIPLINE

Topics	*Most Likely Techniques*
1. Are school and home working at cross purposes? If so, how?	1. Group discussion (two or three groups meet simultaneously depending on number of persons attending).
2. What are the areas for better cooperation?	2. Colloquy (school personnel and Prof. Taylor serve as resource persons; parents serve as audience representatives).
3. What steps can we take first?	3. Panel (parents and school personnel serve as panel members).
	4. Forum (entire group dis-

cusses together, with Prof. Taylor and school personnel as resource persons).

Principal Resources	Goals
1. The members of the learning group.	1. To encourage the school personnel and parents to understand themselves better.
2. School personnel.	
3. Prof. Taylor.	2. To identify specific ways to promote home and school cooperation and understanding in the application of disciplinary measures.

The committee decides to have discussion groups followed by a forum. Two or three groups (depending on the total attendance) will discuss topics number 1 and 2 simultaneously in separate rooms. Prof. Taylor will circulate among the groups as a resource person. Then the moderator of the forum will report to the total group about conclusions reached in the discussion groups concerning these two topics. The total group will then discuss topic number 3 under the guidance of a moderator (the forum). During the forum, Prof. Taylor and a teacher will serve as resource people. The educational techniques (group discussion and forum) are selected because:

1. The topics indicate discussion;
2. The entire group should be able to discuss them intelligently by the third meeting;
3. Trained leaders are available for the discussion groups;
4. The necessary physical arrangements can be made for both the forum and the discussion groups;
5. These techniques seem appropriate to help achieve the goals.

Step 6. *Outlining each activity and the responsibilities to be carried out.*

a. *The outline and timetable.* In the outline and timetable that follow, it is assumed that the necessary leadership and resource persons for the various techniques have been contacted and are willing to serve during the Institute.

21

1st Meeting

Wednesday, January 10, 7:30-9:30 p.m.

Time	Topic or Event	Purpose-Goal	Leadership and Resource People	Technique
7:30 p.m.	Introduction	1. To provide an overview of the Institute. 2. To encourage active participation in the Institute.	The Institute Coordinator (a parent who has been a member of the planning committee)	Speech
7:45 p.m.	"The Meaning of Discipline"	1. To encourage parents and teachers to clarify their thinking about discipline. 2. To promote home-school cooperation regarding discipline.	Moderator (Dr. Jones, Chairman of the Program Committee) Resource Person (Prof. Taylor, Professor of Education) Audience Representatives —2 teachers (names) —2 parents (names)	Colloquy
9:20 p.m.	Written Evaluation	1. To try to improve the group's performance.	Coordinator	
9:25 p.m.	Concluding Remarks	1. To encourage study between meetings. 2. To review the goals of the Institute and the content of the next two meetings.	Coordinator	Speech
9:30 p.m.	Adjourn—(distribute pamphlet to the participants)			

2ND MEETING

Wednesday, January 17, 7:30-9:30 p.m.

Time	Topic or Event	Purpose-Goal	Leadership and Resource People	Technique
7:30 p.m.	Introduction	1. To review the first meeting. 2. To review the goals and characteristics of the entire Institute.	Coordinator	Speech
7:40 p.m.	"Discipline in Our School"	1. To encourage parents and teachers to clarify their ideas and opinions about discipline.	Moderator (Prof. Taylor) Panel Members —3 teachers —the principal	Panel with audience divided into two listening groups (parents in one group, school personnel in another)
8:30 p.m.	"What are the home and school responsibilities regarding discipline?"	1. To clarify responsibilities regarding discipline.	Moderator (Prof. Taylor) Resource Persons (those who served as panel members)	Forum
9:20 p.m.	Written Evaluation	1. To try to improve the group's performance.	Coordinator	
9:25 p.m.	Concluding Remarks	1. To encourage study between meetings. 2. To summarize some of the ideas emerging from the first two meetings.	Coordinator	Speech
9:30 p.m.	Adjourn			

23

3rd Meeting

Wednesday, January 24, 7:30-9:30 p.m.

Time	Topic or Event	Purpose-Goal	Leadership and Resource People	Technique
7:30 p.m.	Introduction	1. To review the first two meetings. 2. To encourage active participation by those present.	Coordinator	Speech
7:35 p.m.	"School-Home Relations and Discipline" (3 discussion groups)	1. To identify specific ways to promote home and school cooperation in the disciplining of children. 2. To encourage the participants to understand themselves and their relationship to the problem.	Trained leaders for each group Prof. Taylor circulates among the groups as resource person	Group Discussion (3 groups meet simultaneously and discuss the same topic).
8:30 p.m.	"What Are the Areas for Better Cooperation?" "What Steps Can We Take First?"	1. To pool the ideas that emerged in the discussion groups. 2. To encourage post-Institute study and action.	Moderator (Dr. Jones, Chairman of the Planning Committee) Resource Persons (Prof. Taylor, the principal, the P.T.A. president)	Forum: (1) moderator reads suggestions coming from discussion groups, (2) general discussion by all persons participating.

3RD MEETING (Continued)

Wednesday, January 24, 7:30-9:30 p.m.

Time	Topic or Event	Purpose-Goal	Leadership and Resource People	Technique
9:20 p.m.	Written Evaluation	1. To help improve future learning activities.	Coordinator	
9:25 p.m.	Summary and Concluding Remarks	1. To pull together some ideas that have emerged. 2. To encourage post-Institute study and action.	Coordinator	Speech
9:30 p.m.	Adjourn			

The chairman calls the committee's attention to the fact that in each case their selection of techniques has been based on the following factors: (1) the group's size and characteristics; (2) the uses, advantages, and limitations of the technique; (3) the topics to be treated and the goals to be achieved; (4) the available resources; (5) the available physical facilities; and (6) the availability of competent leadership.

b. *The responsibilities still to be carried out:*

(1) *Preparing for follow-up study and action.* Despite satisfaction with its planning thus far, the committee is still concerned about two matters: (a) how to establish communication between the participants in the Institute and the members of the association who do not attend, and (b) how best to reach their goal "to identify opportunities for more study and action concerning home and school cooperation." They wish to share some of the benefits of the Institute with those who do not attend and they wish to capitalize on the teamwork and cooperation generated during the Institute. To help accomplish these ends they decide to request time at the regular monthly meeting of the association to present some of the key ideas that emerge from the Institute. Through the cooperation of the program chairman and the president of the association permission is obtained for a 40-minute presentation during the February meeting of the organization. (This session will be planned after the Institute.)

The Institute planning committee then decides to appoint three "content observers" who will seek to identify opportunities for more study and action during the Institute. These observers will write the ideas and suggestions that emerge and are within the concern of home-school cooperation. At the close of the Institute they may be asked to read their suggestions. Or they may wait until after the Institute when they have had a chance to compare notes and test their ideas with P.T.A. officers and school personnel. The observers may serve as the nucleus of a committee designed to exploit the benefits of the Institute and see that the learning leads to further learning opportunities, action, and improvement of the relationships in general.

(2) *Choosing a theme.* It is decided to use "Disciplining Our-

selves and the Children" as the theme for the Institute. This theme should stimulate the interest of the participants and remind them that self-understanding is an important factor in discipline.

(3) *Preparing a printed program.* The committee discusses the need for distributing a printed program to arouse interest in the Institute. Some members feel that printed programs will not be necessary. The final decision, however, is that programs will be used. One teacher agrees to prepare the initial copy of the program, basing it on the schedule for each session; another assumes responsibility for the mimeographing of the program, after getting permission from the principal to use school materials and equipment for the job.

(4) *Obtaining materials.* A member of the planning committee agrees to get the necessary number of copies of the free pamphlet and distribute them at the first meeting.

(5) *Preparing for evaluation.* As the outline of the program and timetable show, the committee has set aside five minutes at each meeting for written evaluation by the participants. It is decided that post-meeting reaction sheets will *not* be used to obtain the desired information. Rather, each participant will be given paper and pencil and asked to make any comment that he desires about each meeting. The planning committee member who has agreed to serve as coordinator for the Institute accepts responsibility for collecting and analyzing this information. He will prepare a summary of his findings for an evaluation meeting of the committee to be held soon after the Institute. The committee members will then discuss the reaction of the participants and their own impressions in the light of the goals set for the Institute.

(6) *Arranging the facilities.* It is decided that responsibilities for audience comfort and the physical set-up need not be carried out by a member of the planning committee. A P.T.A. member expected to be at the Institute will be responsible for this task. A member of the planning committee agrees to contact this person and instruct him about how to arrange the tables and chairs, what room temperature is desirable, and where to place the registration table.

(7) *Instructing those with educational responsibilities.* The committee now examines the outline and timetable to discover

which persons will need instructions in advance of the Institute. The Institute coordinator is reasonably clear about his responsibilities since he was a member of the planning committee. The same is true of Dr. Jones who is to moderate the colloquy at the first meeting and the forum at the third meeting. Dr. Jones agrees to instruct the resource persons participating in the colloquy and the forum and to see that Prof. Taylor receives an honorarium. Another committee member agrees to instruct the moderator and panel members for the panel-forum at the second meeting. Another agrees to instruct the discussion leaders and resource person for the third meeting. (Elsewhere in this book will be found information about instructing persons having educational responsibilities in the techniques to be used at the Institute.)

(8) *Arranging for publicity.* Since the Lincoln School P.T.A. has a publicity chairman, it is decided to ask her to handle newspaper publicity for the Institute. A member of the planning committee agrees to ask her and to see the principal about sending printed announcements home with the children. Another kind of announcement is to be made at the next monthly P.T.A. meeting since one will be held before the Institute. (It will be necessary to clear this with the P.T.A. president.)

(9) *Encouraging advance study.* No advance study will be suggested to those participating in the Institute. The pamphlet "Discipline and the Elementary School Child" will be distributed by the coordinator at the close of the first meeting. The coordinator will encourage the Institute participants to read the pamphlet carefully before the second meeting.

(10) *Preparing for registration.* A P.T.A. member who is not on the planning committee will be asked to supervise registration. The planning committee decides (a) what information to obtain from each registrant; (b) whether or not to use name badges; (c) the specific tasks of all persons involved in registration; and (d) who is to be responsible for any fees that are collected. It is decided to assess each participant a registration fee of 25¢.

VI. An Analysis of the Example

A. *In terms of identifying educational needs and interests*

define the problem

1. *Why begin with needs and interests?* We have seen that the six-step planning procedure begins with the discovery of interests and needs of those persons expected to participate in the learning activity. It is essential to give people opportunities to identify their interests and needs to help motivate them to participate actively. With guidance and training, adults are capable of sharing in the development of the activities planned with them. When the participants are consulted about their educational needs and interests, they tend to accept responsibility for the learning venture.

Persons inexperienced in planning often begin with techniques or resources. That is, they select *how* information is to be acquired and goals achieved before they determine *what* is to be learned and achieved. Logic dictates that we determine how to achieve something after deciding what to achieve. This is why we begin the planning process with the consideration of needs and interests.

2. *Some characteristics of interests and needs.* An interest can be something the participants would like to learn about or come to understand better. We hear people say, "I am interested in world affairs," or "I am interested in knowing about mental health." They may be identifying an interest which can serve as a basis for planning.

A need (educational) is characterized by a lack or deficiency that can be satisfied through learning experiences. We seek activities through which we can satisfy the needs we feel. Needs and interests are interrelated. Interests usually point toward needs. An interest is usually the expression of a need we feel. When our needs and interests coincide we are usually motivated toward a learning experience.

It is often said that a key to successful adult education is the situation or problem-centered approach. The adult tends to see life as a series of problems or obstacles he must overcome or with which he learns to live. He is usually more likely to involve himself in a learning activity centered in problems than in organized subject matter like psychology, history, economics, etc. Thus, problems—undesirable conditions or obstacles—often provide a starting point in helping adults to identify their educational needs and interests.

Adult educators identify and describe various kinds of needs. It is useful to differentiate between a felt need and a real need. The need for distinction is based on the idea that a person frequently cannot tell which is felt and which is real. Sometimes the need he feels is likely to be something he mistakes for a real need. The astute adult educator can often be of help to these persons by helping the participants properly to identify their needs.

Another useful term is the symptomatic need. This refers to the manifestation of a need which the originator considers real but which may be merely a clue to a real need.

When asked to identify their needs, adults often mention something broad, general, or impersonal. For example, an industrial foreman has been having difficulties with some of the men he supervises. He may need to learn to understand himself in relation to the men with whom he works. But often he will identify his need as the developing of a smoother working system or the selecting of better personnel. We often try to resist recognizing our real needs. We sometimes prefer to deal with vague or impersonal symptomatic needs. This may be because we have not learned that cooperative educational experiences can produce desirable group and personal change. We talk about planning a program but not about deliberately changing our behavior. Yet a factor in program planning is an attempt to change our behavior in a desirable direction through legitimate learning experiences.

We cannot always definitely distinguish a real need from a symptomatic need. Often we must proceed on the basis of a need the participants have identified. We must begin where people are. This idea recognizes the learner's present intellectual and emotional condition as the logical starting point for an attempt to help him grow and mature.

3. *The P.T.A. example analyzed.* In the example described above we saw the occasion for planning learning activities arise

30

out of a problem—a disciplinary problem. As soon as parents and school personnel began disputing about discipline, they became part of the problem. When the dust settled a bit, they recognized a need—a need to learn more about discipline. As the planning committee worked through the six-step planning procedure, there emerged the awareness of other needs besides *intellectual* understanding of the concept "Discipline." The committee members began to realize that the P.T.A. members— parents and school personnel—needed to learn to work together and to try to understand each other. They had known about this before they began this process. (The stated goals of P.T.A. stress cooperation.) However, this deep, real need must constantly be rediscovered.

Thus, properly working through the six-step planning procedure tends to insure that programs will be centered in the real needs of the participants. The planning committee's task can be thought of as gradually moving from interests and felt or symptomatic needs toward fulfilling real needs. *When the learning activity is conducted, almost the same condition will exist:* the participants frequently will not want to expose their real needs. But if the program has been carefully planned, if the proper resources and techniques are used, and if the leadership is skillful and patient, a climate will develop in which the participants will feel free to reveal their real needs and receive educational help. Sometimes the revealing of our real needs is deferred until after the learning activity has been conducted. The learning activity or its evaluation can awaken us to the recognition of a real need that we can satisfy by further study or action.

Thus, the entire educational process—planning, conducting, evaluation, follow-up—can be seen as a movement from broad, impersonal interests and felt needs toward the identification and satisfaction of real needs that gradually emerge. This process requires skilled and patient leadership and useful resources. It is not a magical process that comes about because people are meeting in groups. We saw in the P.T.A. example that (a) the planning committee was led by a person who had training in program planning; (b) the Institute involved the use of an outside resource person who had expert knowledge about the topics to be considered; and (c) that learning situations were carefully designed to encourage the learner to recognize his needs and desire to change.

4. *Ways to discover needs and interests.*

a. *Conducting interviews.** Informally questioning some of the persons expected to participate can uncover some needs and interests. Sometimes the persons interviewed are given free rein to suggest any problem, issue, need, interest, or subject that they would like to see discussed or learn more about. Sometimes they are asked to state their preferences from among several choices. It is usually advisable to use more than one interviewer in order to:

(1) Insure against hearing only what you want to hear;
(2) Get a wide selection of interests and needs;
(3) Actively involve several persons in the planning.

It is often useful to ask each person interviewed what problems he would like to overcome (rather than what he thinks his educational needs are).

b. *Circulating a check list.* A brief check list of suggested educational needs and interests can be circulated among (or mailed to) all or part of the potential participants. This allows the participant to choose among several suggested needs and interests. Since the check list greatly restricts the possible responses of those filling it out, it is most effective when used to narrow down the participants' interests and needs after they have previously had an opportunity to identify broad areas of interest and need. For example, if a group has expressed interest in learning about current world affairs they can be asked to make a final choice among: The United Nations, U.S. Foreign Policy in the Middle East, Far Eastern Tensions, and Inter-Nation Cooperative Agreements in Europe.

c. *Taking a problem census.* During a learning activity, the participants can be asked to identify needs and interests for future activities. This is usually done at the close of a meeting. The group can be divided into small groups of six to eight persons

---

* The word *interview* is used here in a different sense from its use described as an educational technique in Chapter 3.

32

(buzz sessions). Each group appoints a leader and talks together for 10 to 20 minutes about interests, needs, topics, subjects, problems, and issues they would like to recommend for future meetings. Each group is encouraged to make one or two recommendations, or the groups can be asked to choose among several needs which have emerged while the meeting was in progress.

d. *Using observers.* In the P.T.A. example we saw how the planning committee used observers to identify needs for further study and action. These observers were not to concern themselves with the learning *process* but rather with the *content* of the Institute. As the Institute was conducted, they were to make a list of some emerging problems which needed further study and action.

e. *By informal discussion and observation.* Sometimes the person in charge of the program can speak to a number of concerned people over a period of time and thereby gather considerable information which can help him to develop a program based on need.

5. *When needs and interests have been prescribed.* Many times we find ourselves starting the planning process with a need or interest already prescribed. For example, many clubs and organizations follow a yearly program in which the main topic, theme, or subject for each meeting has been selected in advance by a national headquarters or a writer of materials. The six-step planning procedure is also applicable to these conditions. When the interest or need is predetermined, the planning then begins at Step 2—developing topics by breaking down the interest or need into the specific problems, issues, questions, or concepts with which the learning activity will be concerned. If both the interest or need (Step 1) and the topics (Step 2) are prescribed, planning can begin with the setting of goals (Step 3). In other words, the six-step procedure is a flexible framework that can be used in part or in its entirety.

B. The P.T.A. example analyzed in terms of goal-setting and evaluation

The setting of goals helps us to remember that something should result from our educational programs. We usually admit that programs ought to lead somewhere—to something more than mere words. But our groups tend to avoid doing anything about it. When asked to set goals, people often say, "We all know why we are planning the program. Why take the time to write down our reasons?" This reluctance often stems from fear of publicly admitting the confusion we feel. Setting goals is painful. It is easier to remain vague than to accept responsibility for planning adult education activities designed to achieve specific results.

1. *What are some characteristics of goals?* Goals selected for adult education activities tend to fall into two general classifications: (a) those which give specific direction to planning what will happen at the meeting and assist in the planning of the learning situation, and (b) those which set forth desirable anticipated results. The latter might be called outcome goals. The former are allied to purposes and are often called task goals. A task goal helps us to decide which topics to emphasize, which resources and techniques to employ. An outcome goal focuses attention on the changes that the program is designed to bring about—usually changes in behavior of the persons participating.

Goals are related to needs and often arise out of needs. A goal might be described as a specific statement of the intention to meet a need.

Goals always stand in relation to a value system or a set of assumptions about what we believe. Usually this value system is implicit. In the P.T.A. example, we saw the committee select this goal: "To Promote Home-School Cooperation Regarding Discipline." It is clear that those who selected this goal place value on cooperation. Cooperation is held to be desirable, and therefore part of the value system of those who stressed it.

Many times a goal is inappropriate because we are starting from an undesirable value or assumption. For example, a committee was planning a program about the "Redevelopment of a Portion of Our Community." The theme of the meeting was to be "Is Redevelopment Necessary?" This goal was proposed: "to learn how we can prevent redevelopment." After intense and frank discussion, the committee came to the conclusion that the goal should read as follows: "To identify in ourselves obstacles to objectivity in considering redevelopment." This committee recognized a need to change values underlying the goal that first seemed desirable.

34

2. *Criteria for effective goals.*

a. Goals should be realistic and specific. It should be reasonable to hope that a particular goal can be achieved. If goals are merely remote desires, rather than anticipated outcomes, they do not motivate the learner. Rather than broad generalities, goals should be expressed in clear-cut, understandable language. For example, "to encourage further study" is vague, while "to motivate at least 50 per cent of our group to buy and read one pamphlet" is specific.

b. The learner or participant should share in choosing the goals. True, this is not always possible. However, opportunities to encourage the participants to share in selecting goals are frequently overlooked. Planning by a representative committee should not be accepted as the only substitute. The planning procedure can usually be interrupted long enough to permit the expected participants to express preferences and become involved in selecting goals. When a learner has helped to identify and select goals that will produce a change in behavior, he is more likely to understand the need for and nature of behavioral change.

c. Good goals are expressed in terms of behavior as well as in terms of knowledge to be acquired. One goal set by the planning committee in the P.T.A. example was "to identify opportunities for more study and action concerning home and school cooperation." This goal can only be achieved in terms of people *doing* something about it. Someone will have to follow up to see if this occurs. Thus, this goal should be useful for evaluation purposes.

3. *Goals and evaluation.* Educational evaluation is concerned with judging the extent to which constructive learning takes place. In one sense of the word, evaluation goes on throughout the planning and conducting of a learning activity; people are continually making judgments about the worth of their learning experiences together. However, a more precise use of the term "evaluation" restricts it to conscious, organized attempts by the teacher-leaders, the planning committee, or the entire learning group to measure the extent to which the learning goals have been achieved. Results are measurable only in terms of the desired outcomes. Thus, thorough-going evaluation involves measurement and testing. Few adult groups are now equipped to do

this. However, there is a great deal to be gained from approaching evaluation in a more systematic and objective way than we usually do.

4. *Ways to get information for evaluating.*

a. *Post-meeting reaction sheets.* It is now common practice to have participants fill out a brief questionnaire at the close of an educational program or meeting. In the case of a single program, the term "Post-Meeting Reaction Sheet" is often used, saving the term "questionnaire" for a series of programs. Throughout Chapters 3 and 4 of this book are examples of check lists that can be adapted for obtaining post-meeting reactions.

b. *3 x 5 cards.* One or two revealing questions can be answered on a 3 x 5 card. For example, participants can tell what part of the program they found most useful. Be sure to ask significant questions which are carefully worded. A question such as "What is the most useful idea you got from the program?" or "Which ideas seemed to apply to your own problems?" will get a better answer than "How did you like the program?" Cards are easy to handle and can be placed on chairs before a meeting starts.

c. *Interview.* People can often be questioned informally about their reactions before they leave a meeting or telephoned after they have had time to reflect about it. Important here is the fact that the interviewer must know what he wishes to learn. He will need a list of questions, even though he may not show these questions to the person he is interviewing.

d. *Observer.* One or more persons can have the job of studying a learning situation as it unfolds. Like the interviewer, the observer must clearly understand what he is looking for. He might gather data about (1) the way certain duties are performed (e.g., chairman, panel moderator), (2) the appropriateness of resources in relation to the topics and goals, and (3) the way the participants reacted to various parts of the program.

e. *Participants discuss program.* At the close of a meeting the participants can be asked for their reactions by having small discussion groups, or through a kind of committee-of-the-whole discussion. Discussion should be carefully planned with regard to time and purpose. Failure to do this may result in (1) superficial remarks, bouquet throwing, or buck passing, (2) loss of the en-

36

thusiasm engendered by the program, or (3) hurt feelings. Despite these dangers, discussion can be profound and revealing.

f. *Planning committee critique.* A planning committee can convene immediately after a program for the purpose of comparing notes and discussing how well the program was conducted. They should avoid letting their critique seem to be a closed club meeting to talk about people.

5. *Evaluation as a series of steps.* The following procedure may be a helpful way of thinking about evaluation. It is a series of steps that can be begun as soon as the goals for a learning activity have been set.

a. *Break down each goal into specific outcomes.* These anticipated results should be stated as clearly as possible and expressed in specific terms.

b. *Decide what information or evidence would be helpful in judging the extent to which the goals have been achieved.* For example, suppose a goal was to motivate a group of women to undergo physical examinations regularly. Evaluation would require information about the frequency with which each woman participating underwent physical examinations *before* and *after* the learning experience which is being evaluated.

c. *Decide where, when, and how to get the information you need.* This usually means developing questionnaires, planning interviews, critiques, observations, etc. In the case of the example just cited, physicians' records could provide the necessary information.

d. *Obtain, tabulate, and summarize the needed information.* After obtaining the information, it is helpful to draw up summaries of the findings for convenient use of those involved in the evaluation.

e. *Interpret the information obtained.* Make judgments about the extent to which the goals were achieved. Try to be as objective as possible when making these judgments. Try to avoid the temptation to find what you hope to find regardless of the evidence.

f. *Act on the findings.* Decide what action is appropriate. What new learning activities are needed? Inform those who participated in evaluation what you have learned and how they were helpful.

In the P.T.A. example we saw that the planning committee set definite learning goals and that these goals were specific enough to lend themselves to evaluation of results. When the committee reached Step 6 in the planning process, one member took responsibility for guiding the evaluation of the Institute being planned. It was decided to base its evaluation on the impressions of the planning committee and on information obtained from the participants at the end of each meeting. After the Institute, the committee would make judgments regarding the extent to which the goals were achieved.

The person in charge of evaluation did the following:

1. Insisted that the planning committee make its goals specific enough to permit evaluation;

2. Prevailed upon the planning committee to set a specific date for evaluating the Institute;

3. Developed a post-meeting reaction sheet to be distributed at each session of the Institute;

4. Arranged to have the post-meeting reaction sheets reproduced in quantity, distributed, and collected at each meeting (working closely with the Institute coordinator);

5. Tabulated the information obtained on the post-meeting reaction sheets and summarized the information, reproducing it in quantity for the evaluation meeting of the planning committee after the Institute;

6. Served as a resource person at the evaluation meeting of the planning committee;

7. Took initiative to see that appropriate action resulted from the evaluation sessions.

C. The P.T.A. example analyzed in terms of topics, resources, and techniques

We said that topics are the specific problems, issues, questions, and concepts that the learning activity will treat. They represent statements describing the content of the program to be conducted. Each meeting or session usually treats several topics.

We saw the P.T.A. planning committee list topics rapidly on the chart pad in their own language. They set down questions and issues as they saw them. They did not merely have an expert come to the P.T.A. and talk about discipline in *his* terms.

When they examined their topics they found that they fell into three broad categories:

> The Meaning of Discipline
> Discipline in Our School
> School-Home Relationships and Discipline

These three categories formed the basis for the three sessions of the Institute.

Further examination of the topics reveals that (1) some are requests for factual information (e.g. What is discipline?), while others are (2) matters of opinion (e.g. Are school personnel in general agreement?), or (3) issues that invite discussion (e.g. What are areas for better cooperation?).

The planning committee faced the task of selecting techniques that lend themselves to the exploration and management of the topics at hand. An example: for the third meeting they needed a technique that would be suitable for discussing and identifying "Areas for Better Cooperation." Had they chosen a speech—by the principal or their outside resource person, Prof. Taylor—the audience would have heard one man's opinion as to areas for better cooperation. But one goal for the session was to promote better home-school cooperation regarding discipline. Thus it seemed essential to involve the audience in identifying the areas of cooperation *if the audience was expected to act* as a result of the learning activity.

The forum is a technique for involving a large audience in discussion. It requires a competent moderator, one or more resource persons and audience members who have enough knowledge about the topic to discuss it effectively. All of these conditions could be met. The forum was selected because it was the appropriate technique:

1. In terms of *topics* (content to be treated),
2. In terms of the *goals* that had been set,
3. In terms of *resources* available,
4. In terms of available *leadership,*
5. In terms of the characteristics of the audience or *participants* to be involved in the learning experience,
6. In terms of its own *characteristics as a technique.*

VII. Resumé of Factors to Consider When Selecting Adult Education Procedures

A. *The learner or participant*

His needs and interests; his background: vocational, cultural, educational; the extent of his knowledge about what is to be learned; his age and physical condition. Also important are the learner's expectations: how he looks on the learning experience intended for him. Important, too, is the size of the group to be involved. Certain procedures work most effectively with larger groups, others with smaller groups. The average age of the group members must be taken into consideration. Older persons often have physiological handicaps (vision, hearing) which must be taken into account. Persons planning adult education experiences should constantly answer this question: "What kind of a person am I working with?"

B. *The physical environment*

The setting should be an appropriate one for adults and for the specific activities to be conducted. Some procedures require a specific physical arrangement.

C. *The leadership available*

Qualified leadership and guidance is essential. Many procedures require specific leadership skills if they are to be used successfully.

D. *The topics, goals, and resources*

That is, *what* we wish to learn, *why* we wish to learn it, and *who* or *what* can help us learn.

E. *The characteristics of the procedure to be used*

Its nature, its uses, its advantages and limitations, and its pattern of communication.

F. *The institution—its expectations and concerns*

Sometimes the goals and the expectations of the institution (i.e. the school, church, industry, etc.) are either different than those of some of the persons who are members of the institution, or are not mutually understood. The procedures selected should be appropriate to the task of assisting participants to identify the possibility of these differences as well as understanding them.

The next three chapters describe the characteristics of various adult education procedures.

CHAPTER 3

Fourteen Educational Techniques

The adult educator, or persons responsible for planning a learning activity, must arrange learners and resources in such a way as seems best suited to the acquiring of information, the exchange of views, or whatever learnings are desired. Thus the adult educator *structures* the learning situation. He decides what patterns of learning procedures will be appropriate and how people can be encouraged to interact with each other. One type of structure—panel, or speech, or field trip, etc.—is called a technique.

As we have seen in Chapter 2, techniques should be carefully chosen. No one technique is suited to all situations. We must carefully diagnose our educational problem before selecting a technique.

The techniques described in this chapter are not finite and inflexible. They can be adjusted and adapted to the situation at hand. The skillful adult educator adapts and modifies these basic techniques and uses them in many combinations so that he has almost endless possibilities for the different situations that confront him.

One way to modify or adapt a technique is through the use of appropriate subtechniques outlined in Chapter 4.

I. Colloquy

A. What is a colloquy?

A colloquy is a modification of the panel using six or eight persons—three or four representing the audience and three or four resource persons or experts (if only one resource person is available, proceed with him). A moderator directs the proceedings. The colloquy members, selected from and representing the audience, ask questions, express opinions, and raise issues to be treated by the resource persons (experts). The general audience listens, but occasionally they may participate under the guidance of the moderator.

B. *When should the colloquy be used?*

The colloquy may be the correct technique to use when topics and goals point toward doing one or more of the following:

1. Stimulating interest in a topic;
2. Identifying, clarifying, or solving problems;
3. Identifying and exploring issues;
4. Bringing expert knowledge to bear on problems and needs as they emerge from discussion;
5. Giving the audience opportunities to understand the component parts of a topic;
6. Weighing the advantages and disadvantages of a course of action;
7. Reducing the natural barriers that usually stand between a large audience and resource persons, thereby helping to establish rapport between the audience and those on the platform;
8. Offering resource persons the opportunity to get a clear picture of the audience's knowledge of the topic(s).

C. *Who are the personnel involved?*

1. *The moderator* is the person who guides the discussion of the resource persons, the audience representatives, and the audience. He is skilled in the use of techniques of discussion and stimulating participation in a large audience. He should be able to guide the discussion in such a way as to take advantage of the flexibility of this technique.

2. *The resource persons* are usually one to four persons chosen for their particular knowledge and interest in the subject to be discussed and their ability to participate in an informal way.

3. *The audience representatives* are chosen for their interest in the topics and their ability to ask questions and make intelligent comments so as to clarify the topics for themselves and the audience. They can be chosen in advance by the planning committee or during the meeting.

4. *The audience* is usually composed of persons interested in the topic(s). Their presence at the meeting is an indication of

some interest. Their intellectual levels and interests will vary considerably. However, it is essential to adapt the program to the needs and interests of the audience.

If controversial issues are involved, many of the audience members will have made up their minds one way or another before they come to the meeting. Some know very little if anything about the topic(s) and others are well informed. The group may contain persons who are unable to relate the topic(s) to their own experience. Another part of the audience may be persons who know something about the topic(s) to be discussed but have not come to any definite conclusions.

The character and amount of the participation often depends on:

a. The original interest and that which may be stimulated during the meeting;

b. The skill of the moderator in handling the discussion;

c. The knowledge of the audience about the topic(s) under discussion;

d. The ability and willingness of the resource persons to answer the questions sympathetically and understandably.

D. What is the usual pattern of communication?

It is important to know something about the normal flow of verbal participation when the colloquy is used. The diagram below shows that there can be verbal participation by all—the moderator, each resource person, each audience representative,

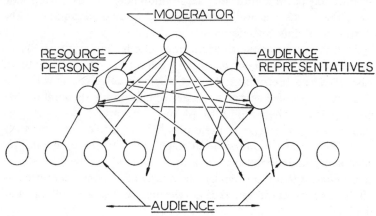

and the audience. It also shows that the audience's contributions are usually routed through the moderator and that the greater part of the verbal participation will usually be between the resource persons and the audience representatives. The latter do not necessarily route their contributions through the moderator.

E. Advantages and limitations of the colloquy

1. Advantages:

a. The colloquy permits a large audience to be represented and also offers them some opportunity for direct participation;

b. Audience representatives can get clarification if a vague or abstract statement is made by the resource person;

c. Resource persons tend to consider carefully the problems and needs of the audience;

d. The colloquy encourages the audience to feel responsibility for their representatives and therefore to listen and participate actively;

e. The natural barriers that usually stand between audience and resource persons tend to be reduced with this technique;

f. The colloquy permits considerable flexibility in the learning situation since the moderator can guide discussion toward topics of concern as they emerge.

2. Limitations:

a. Experienced moderators who understand the functioning of the colloquy are not always available;

b. The audience and its representatives may not be sufficiently informed to ask meaningful questions of the resource persons;

c. The audience members may hesitate to participate actively;

d. The resource persons are not always willing to listen to the questions and make their remarks relatively brief and to the point.

F. Check list for appraising the colloquy

This check list can be used as a help in deciding whether or not the colloquy is an appropriate technique to use for a particular adult learning situation. If the answers tend to be "no" or "undecided," consider using another technique.

	Yes	No	Unde-cided

1. Do topics and goals point toward the need for a technique with a great deal of flexibility? ＿＿ ＿＿ ＿＿

2. Would this technique help to reduce the barriers between resource persons and the audience? ＿＿ ＿＿ ＿＿

3. Would the use of a colloquy encourage resource persons to consider carefully the needs and interests of the audience? ＿＿ ＿＿ ＿＿

4. Is reluctance to participate expected (so that the presence of the audience representatives may help to encourage verbal participation by the group as a whole)? ＿＿ ＿＿ ＿＿

5. Is the audience expected to be so large as to make representation advisable? ＿＿ ＿＿ ＿＿

6. Will the use of audience representatives stimulate interest on the part of the audience? ＿＿ ＿＿ ＿＿

7. Are resource persons available who:

a. Are well-grounded in their field? ＿＿ ＿＿ ＿＿
b. Can operate flexibly in an informal manner? ＿＿ ＿＿ ＿＿
c. Can make direct, brief comments? ＿＿ ＿＿ ＿＿

8. Is a moderator available who has the following qualifications:

a. Has enough knowledge about the topic and goals? ＿＿ ＿＿ ＿＿
b. Can instruct the audience representatives and resource persons? ＿＿ ＿＿ ＿＿
c. Can promote effective discussion? ＿＿ ＿＿ ＿＿
d. Can encourage participation by audience members? ＿＿ ＿＿ ＿＿
e. Understands the colloquy as a technique? ＿＿ ＿＿ ＿＿
f. Can remain neutral and show interest? ＿＿ ＿＿ ＿＿

46

9. Are qualified audience representatives available?

_____ _____ _____

10. Can the necessary physical set-up be made?

_____ _____ _____

11. Are there other techniques that might be more appropriate choices?

_____ _____ _____

If yes, what are they and why? _____

_____

_____

G. *What are the responsibilities of the colloquy members?*

1. *What does the moderator do?*

a. *Prior to the colloquy,* the moderator:

(1) Plans for physical arrangements that will aid informal discussion and problem solving;

(2) Has clearly in mind the topics to be dealt with and the desired goals;

(3) Carefully studies the characteristics of the group that is anticipated. He considers the age, sex, background, and points of view of the audience: What will they have in common? In what respects will their interest in and knowledge of the topic(s) vary? What are the implications of all this for the conducting of the colloquy and for orienting the resource persons?

(4) Plans for audience participation and determines the point in discussion at which the audience will be invited to participate verbally;

(5) Plans and carries out steps to encourage advanced reading and follow-up study;

(6) Gets acquainted with the resource persons, and the audience representatives* explaining the following to them:

(a) The topic(s) to be covered and the goal(s) to be reached,

---

* Sometimes the audience representatives are selected only a few minutes before the beginning of the colloquy. In this case it may be possible to give them a brief orientation. When instructing audience representatives under these conditions, stress the mechanics of the colloquy and explain exactly what is expected of them.

(b) The relationship of this colloquy to other parts of the meeting or series,

(c) The mechanics of the colloquy,

(d) The characteristics of the expected audience and their apparent needs and interests regarding the topics to be considered,

(e) The need for audience representatives to develop some questions and comments to put to the resource persons;

(7) Plans the introduction that he will present at the beginning of the colloquy. This brief presentation should contain the following information:

(a) The topic and goals and their importance—what the audience can expect to gain,

(b) How this colloquy fits in with a larger program, if such is in progress,

(c) How the colloquy works and the responsibilities of all persons involved,

(d) The names and qualifications of the resource persons,

(e) The names of the audience representatives,

(f) The need for active listening,

(g) When and how the audience is to participate,

(h) The amount of time available for the colloquy.

b. *During the colloquy,* the moderator:

(1) Presents his introduction (see above);

(2) Encourages and develops audience participation, at the time decided on for their participation;

(3) Restates and clearly directs the questions asked by the audience representatives and by individuals from the audience to the appropriate resource persons (if necessary). He refrains from entering into the discussion or answering questions;

(4) Tries to develop and maintain a friendly and informal atmosphere;

(5) Recognizes members of the audience one at a time;

(6) Makes practical applications within the knowledge of the audience;

(7) Directs the course of the discussion to fit situations that arise;

(8) Remains neutral if controversy arises;

(9) Tries to prevent a monopoly of talk by one person or a few;

(10) Summarizes when it is necessary:

(a) To avoid destructive conflicts,

(b) To get ready to move on to a new phase in the discussion,

(c) To keep all participants on the topic under discussion,

(d) To clarify when the group seems to be confused.

(11) Allows an appropriate amount of time for each topic under discussion, trying to prevent the discussion from bogging down on one or two topics;

(12) Prevents resource persons from dominating the discussion (*The resource persons may assume a dominant role quite unconsciously* if this danger is not guarded against. In fact, they are often more or less forced into a dominant role due to the failure of other persons present to assume responsibility.);

(13) Suggests follow-up study by all participants if advisable.

2. *What do the resource persons do?*

a. *Prior to the colloquy,* the resource persons:

(1) Familiarize themselves with the colloquy technique;

(2) Study the characteristics of the group expected to be present;

(3) Try to grasp the relationship of the colloquy in which they are to participate to the program (or series of programs) as a whole;

(4) Prepare to participate flexibly and informally;

(5) Prepare to talk about the topics that are likely to emerge. (The audience representatives may have prepared questions in advance that will provide clues to the kind of topics that will arise.)

b. *During the colloquy,* each of the resource persons:

(1) Contributes when his opinion is needed;

(2) Makes *brief,* direct comments appropriate to the questions asked and to the audience represented;

(3) Uses language that the audience understands;

(4) Refrains from using the occasion to promote ideas not directly applicable;

(5) Avoids disparaging remarks about the contributions of the audience representatives and the audience;

(6) Encourages the audience to participate.

3. *What do the audience representatives do?*

a. *Prior to the colloquy,* the audience representatives:

(1) Inform themselves about the purpose and goals of the meeting (or series of meetings);

(2) Inform themselves about the topics to be discussed in the colloquy;

(3) Develop questions and comments to put to the resource persons.

b. *During the colloquy,* the audience representatives:

(1) Present topics—in the form of comments, problems, and questions—to the resource persons;

(2) Ask for clarification and explanation;

(3) Attempt to make their contributions clear and to the point;

(4) Show interest and seek to stimulate audience participation.

4. *What is expected of the audience?*

a. Advanced study or other preparation;

b. Thoughtful listening and verbal participation when called for;

c. Support and encouragement of their representatives;

d. Polite but firm insistence that the moderator, the resource persons, and the audience representatives keep in mind and deal with the concerns of the audience.

H. *Physical arrangements and audience comfort*
1. *Physical set-up.*

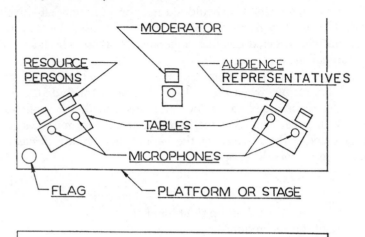

2. *Audience comfort.* Keep the following points in mind when making arrangements:

a. Extremes in temperature are distracting;

b. The audience should be comfortably seated and must not face a glaring light;

c. The audience must be able to see and hear the moderator, the audience representatives, and the resource person (Provide a platform or stage if necessary);

d. Select a room or auditorium appropriate to the size of the group and the character of the meeting;

e. Provide chairs and tables for the moderator, the audience representatives, and the resource persons;

f. Secure a public address system with individual microphones, if necessary, but be sure it is tested before it is used;

g. It may be advisable to use name cards for the moderator, the resource persons, and the audience representatives. A card with *large* lettering enables people at a distance to identify each person on the platform.

I. How to evaluate after the colloquy has been conducted

The following check list should aid in appraising how effectively the colloquy has been conducted. It can be used by (1) the persons who selected this technique and (2) those who take part in the colloquy.

It is useful to have mimeographed or dittoed copies of the check list for use when the colloquy has been concluded.

If the replies tend to be "no" and "undecided," the colloquy may well have been used *ineffectively*, and future mistakes can be avoided if the reasons for the various answers are discussed briefly in a cooperative spirit.

	Yes	No	Unde-cided
1. Was the physical set-up right for effective use of this technique?	____	____	____
2. Was audience comfort provided for?	____	____	____
3. Did the moderator show evidence of having done the following prior to the colloquy:			
a. Planned his introduction carefully?	____	____	____
b. Carefully studied the characteristics of the group as a whole?	____	____	____
4. Did the moderator do the following during the colloquy:			
a. Identify the goals to be achieved?	____	____	____
b. Inform all participants of the nature of the colloquy and their responsibilities?	____	____	____
c. Guide the discussion effectively?	____	____	____
d. Try to avoid or minimize limitations of this technique?	____	____	____
e. Permit anyone to dominate the discussion?	____	____	____
5. Did the resource persons show evidence of understanding their role and their responsibilities?			

a. Did they make brief, direct comments? _____ _____ _____

b. Did they participate flexibly and informally? _____ _____ _____

c. Did they avoid assuming a dominant role? _____ _____ _____

d. Did they use understandable language? _____ _____ _____

e. Did they encourage the audience to participate? _____ _____ _____

6. Did the audience representatives understand their responsibilities?

a. Were they informed about the topics and goals? _____ _____ _____

b. Did they show interest and initiate discussion? _____ _____ _____

c. Did they keep in mind the needs and interests of those they were representing? _____ _____ _____

7. Did the audience members show evidence of having understood their responsibilities?

a. Had they prepared to participate? _____ _____ _____

b. Did they listen attentively? _____ _____ _____

c. Did they join in the discussion? _____ _____ _____

d. Was their verbal participation fairly well-balanced (not dominated by a few members of the audience)? _____ _____ _____

e. Did they support their representatives? _____ _____ _____

f. Did they try to insure that their needs and interests were dealt with by the moderator and the resource persons? _____ _____ _____

8. What was accomplished?

a. Were worthwhile points made in the discussion? _____ _____ _____

b. Did members of the audience show evidence of having acquired information, new viewpoints, or of having changed attitudes? ___ ___ ___

    c. Did the group make progress toward their goals? ___ ___ ___

    d. Have problems or needs emerged which point toward further study or action? ___ ___ ___

    e. Was there evidence of willingness to accept responsibility for further study or action? ___ ___ ___

9. Was the colloquy an appropriate technique for this learning situation? ___ ___ ___

What other techniques might have been effective and why? _____

J. How the colloquy might be used—an example

An adult evening school class of 50 persons is halfway through a semester-long course in "Personal Finance." They are scheduled for a one-hour session on "Wise investments for persons with income on the lower and medium levels." Several well-qualified resource persons (such as a local banker and broker) are available, as are some good reading materials which can be supplied by banks and investment companies.

The instructor in the course wishes to promote active participation by the class members. He feels that they will have problems requiring the aid of qualified resource persons. He can also provide good advance reading material. So the techniques that are sometimes adequate for presenting information (for example, speech and modern symposium) do not seem appropriate. He considers an interview (see p. 106) followed by a forum (see p. 83) but rejects these possibilities in favor of a colloquy, which he will moderate. The colloquy will:

    1. Make use of several *well-qualified* resource persons;

    2. Allow the teacher's knowledge to be used in his job of moderator;

    3. Interest the students by the use of class members as audience representatives;

4. Allow the moderator to get the entire class involved in the discussion (in the latter stages of the colloquy).

II. COMMITTEE

A. *What is the committee?*

A committee is a small group of persons appointed or elected to perform a task that cannot be done efficiently by an entire group or organization, or done effectively by one person.

Not all committees are set up for purely educational purposes, but the success of almost all adult education programs is dependent on the proper functioning of one or more committees. The most common uses of committees in adult education are to plan and evaluate activities and to act in advisory capacity to persons directing programs.

Of the typical committee to be found in the countless organizations in existence in our society, the following can usually be said:

1. The committee is authorized by and responsible to a parent organization—that is, the larger group of which it is a part;
2. The committee members are appointed by the presiding officers or elected by the members of the organization;
3. The powers and duties are fixed by the person making the appointment or by the constitution and by-laws of the organization.

B. *When should the committee be used?*

This technique can be used for the following purposes:

1. To plan a single educational activity, a series, or an entire year's program;
2. To evaluate adult education activities;
3. To act as an advisory body;
4. To study a problem or issue and report the findings;
5. To promote or publicize a program or activity;
6. To make local arrangements for a meeting, workshop, institute, etc.;
7. To reach a conclusion regarding a course of action;
8. To take action, provided that the committee's instructions and authority include action.

C. Who are the personnel involved?

1. *The chairman* is responsible for the mechanics and for reporting the activities or findings to the parent organization. He usually gives more direction and guidance than a discussion leader, but he should not be arbitrary. He offers whatever information and opinion he believes will be helpful.

The chairman should be more interested in the committee's job than in his own importance. He should trust people and seek to bring about the release of their creative energies. A sense of humor is helpful. Above all he should be capable of following through on a job until it is properly completed. The chairman may be appointed by the presiding officer of the parent body, elected by the parent body, or elected by members of the committee.

Sometimes *co-chairmen* are appointed to committees. If co-chairmen are used, care should be taken to see that they are persons who can work well together.

2. *The committee members* should be the persons best qualified to assist in the committee's task. They should be willing to accept responsibility and follow the task through to its completion. They may be chosen or elected both from within and from without the organization. They are not necessarily members of the organization.

The number of persons appointed or elected depends upon the kind of job to be done. Small committees (three or four persons) can usually handle well such a task as writing a constitution or selecting facilities for a meeting. Larger committees (up to 15 persons) are often needed to do research or solve a problem of great concern to an organization. A program planning committee should be broadly representative of the anticipated audience; it usually contains from 6 to 12 members.

3. *Consultants or resource persons* are sometimes appointed to committees or asked by the chairman to join them at specific meetings. They are persons who have specialized knowledge that the committee needs.

4. *An observer* can be used to assist the committee to have discussion that is as productive as possible. The observer watches

the progress of the committee, the participation, and the team-work displayed. When requested, he makes comments and sug-gestions that he believes will assist the group members to work well together and efficiently accomplish their task.

D. What is the usual pattern of communication?

Although a committee is not a discussion group in the technical sense of the term, it should be characterized by verbal participation by all members. The chairman will tend to speak more fre-quently than a discussion leader, but the members are not ex-pected to wait for recognition before speaking. The chairman provides the organization and direction that he feels will result in creativity and productivity. Comments are not necessarily routed through the chairman; however, only one discussion should be in progress at any one time. The following diagram attempts to show how the conversation might flow among the committee members.

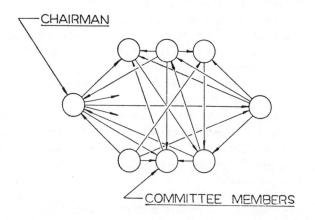

E. Advantages and limitations of the committee

1. Advantages:

a. Appointing a committee spreads responsibility among sev-eral persons;

b. Potential leaders may emerge and gain experience by serv-ing on committees;

c. Work that a large number of persons cannot do efficiently can be done by a committee;

d. The committee can be given the necessary resources and allowed the time for careful exploration and study;

e. This technique can enable an organization to make good use of its members who have special interests and abilities;

f. Several minds are often better than one.

2. *Limitations:*

a. It is sometimes difficult to appoint a group of persons who can work well together;

b. Committee members sometimes live so far apart that they find serving on the committee to be too costly in terms of money or time;

c. The parent organization is sometimes not prepared to define responsibilities and to make use of committee findings or conclusions;

d. It is sometimes difficult to determine whether or not a committee is more appropriate than action by one person or by the group as a whole—inappropriate and unnecessary committees can be set up (Here we must carefully analyze the problem to determine the appropriate technique.);

e. There is sometimes a tendency to draft persons for committee work against their will;

f. Sometimes a person who is a manipulator will select, by one way or another, a committee to do his bidding while appearing to be democratic (for example, appointing a committee without giving it responsibility and encouragement may be a way to see that nothing is done).

F. Check list for decision about a committee

Before setting up a committee consult the following check list. If the answers tend to be "no" and "undecided," the committee probably should not be established.

	Yes	No	Unde-cided

1. Does the parent organization intend to make use of the committee's work?

2. Is the purpose of the committee clearly related to the purposes and goals of the parent organization?

3. Is the task one that can be done more effectively by a small group than by either one person or the organization as a whole?

4. Is a qualified chairman available and willing to serve?

5. Will the chairman be instructed by an officer or other appropriate person in the parent organization?

6. Can the chairman and the committee be given the training or orientation that seems necessary?

7. Will the committee have enough time and resources to do its task?

8. Is consultative assistance available if needed?

9. Are adequate meeting facilities available?

10. Are the appropriate persons willing to serve as committee members so that the committee has broad representation of differing interests and points of view?

G. Responsibilities involved in using the committee

1. *What does the chairman do?*

a. *Prior to the meeting(s),* the chairman:

(1) Makes certain that he understands the purposes for which the committee has been established and its assigned task;

(2) Reviews the aims and purposes of the organization or parent body that has set up the committee;

(3) Prepares necessary information for the committee mem-

bers—information that will aid their understanding of their task and make possible effective discussion and problem solving;

(4) Makes suitable physical arrangements for the meeting(s);

(5) Carefully briefs the committee members regarding the time, place, and date of each meeting;

(6) Develops a tentative agenda—a list of problems and concerns the committee can deal with. Agenda items are solicited from (a) members of the committee and (b) board members and officers of the parent organization;

(7) Determines which agenda items call for discussion by the committee and which ones call for action on his own part or by other persons on the committee;

(8) Prepares introductory remarks that will make clear:

(a) The purpose and task of the committee,

(b) The resources available,

(c) The time available to get the job done,

(d) The responsibilities of the committee members,

(e) The tentative agenda;

b. *During the meeting(s)*, the chairman:

(1) Starts and closes on time;

(2) Makes his introduction (see above);

(3) Sees that committee members get to know one another;

(4) Conducts the discussion, promoting participation by all;*

(5) Assists the group to set goals and define problems;

(6) Makes occasional summaries;

(7) Makes effective use of consultants, resource persons and the observer (if the group needs them);

(8) Makes special assignments for research, fact finding, report writing, and appropriate action steps, appointing appropriate subcommittees (Jobs should be distributed on a basis of interest, ability, and willingness to carry out assignments.);

(9) Encourages the committee members to contribute their time and talent to the task of the committee;

(10) Seeks to maintain a friendly, cooperative atmosphere of teamwork;

---

* In planning to lead a committee meeting, it will be helpful to review also the responsibilities of the leader in group discussion (see p. 99).

(11) Suggests that the committee evaluate its own performance by means of observer reports, questionnaires or open discussion;

(12) Prepares, or sees that there is prepared, a report to the parent body;

(13) Follows up to see that assignments are carried out and that the parent body makes use of the committee's work.

2. *What do the committee members do?* They

a. Assist the chairman by offering suggestions and voluntarily assuming responsibilities;

b. Take part in discussion;

c. Stay on the topic under discussion;

d. Undertake fact-finding or research;

e. Turn in reports on time;

f. Help to analyze problems;

g. Make suggestions for action;

h. Accept responsibility for action.

3. *What obligations does the parent organization have?* The group that sets up the committee should:

a. Appoint only necessary committees;

b. Try to be certain that a committee is the most effective way of accomplishing a particular task;

c. Appoint or elect a qualified chairman who understands and accepts his responsibilities;

d. Provide orientation or, when desirable, training for committee chairmen and members;

e. Make clear the purposes, tasks, and deadlines for the committee, yet allow freedom for creativity on the part of the members of the committee;

f. Give the committee the necessary time and resources to carry out its assignment;

g. Make clear the limits of the committee's authority;

h. Stand ready to make use of the committee's findings or recommendations and to appoint one person (usually an officer) to instruct the committee concerning its responsibilities;

i. Consult the committee before modifying those findings.

H. *Physical arrangements and group comfort*

1. *Physical set-up.*

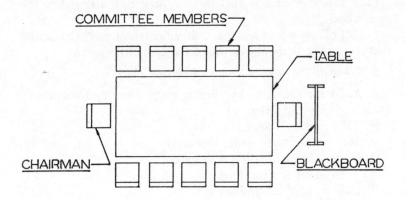

2. *Group comfort.* Keep the following in mind when making arrangements:

a. Arrange for face-to-face seating in which no one faces a glaring light;

b. Provide a blackboard or easel;

c. Provide committee members with paper and pencil and copies of any tables, charts, or similar information that will be helpful;

d. Provide a suitable room free from excessive noise or distraction;

e. Extremes in temperature are distracting;

f. Provide name cards for each committee member, if needed.

I. *How to evaluate a committee*

The following check list will aid the chairman and the committee in looking at the effectiveness of the committee's performance.

Copies of this list can be made and distributed to each committee member.

If the trend of replies is toward "no" and "undecided," the committee chairman should consider possible improvements and consult with officers in the parent organization.

	Yes	No	Unde-cided
1. Do we understand the purpose and tasks of the committee?	___	___	___
2. Do we have adequate meeting facilities including a blackboard?	___	___	___
3. Is a tentative agenda worked out in advance of meetings by the chairman?	___	___	___
4. Does the committee seem to be of appropriate size?	___	___	___
5. Is the discussion effectively led?	___	___	___
6. Do we work as a team?	___	___	___
7. Are the members willing to accept responsibility?	___	___	___
8. Is individual initiative encouraged by the chairman?	___	___	___
9. Is the committee dominated by one or two persons?	___	___	___
10. If resource persons or consultants are used, are they used effectively?	___	___	___
11. Is the available time used efficiently?	___	___	___
12. Are the members all well-acquainted with one another?	___	___	___
13. Do we have the necessary resources to carry out our task?	___	___	___
14. Do we have a sense of accomplishment?	___	___	___

III. DEMONSTRATION

A. What is a demonstration?

A demonstration is a carefully prepared presentation that shows how to perform an act or use a procedure. It is accompanied by appropriate oral and visual explanations, illustrations, and questions.

First the learners watch an expert perform the demonstration and listen to the explanation. Then the demonstration is followed by practice opportunities for the learners. It is sometimes necessary for each group member to practice each step in a procedure immediately after it has been demonstrated under the direction of the demonstrator. (For example: when class members imitate the pronunciation of the person teaching them how to make a particular sound in a foreign language. If the maintenance department of an institution wishes to show its painters a new way to paint window sashes, an expert can demonstrate the new technique before the painters, then supervise each person as he tries to do it.)

Other examples of procedures appropriate for demonstration are: how to introduce a speaker, sell a product, clean a rifle, or lead a discussion. The procedures demonstrated may be very simple or rather complex. The procedures may be demonstrated by one person or a team.

B. When should the demonstration be used?

This technique can be used to:

1. Teach people how to perform an act or use a new procedure or product;

2. Promote confidence that a procedure is feasible for the learner to undertake;

3. Promote interest in learning and use of a procedure.

C. Who are the personnel involved?

1. *The demonstrator* plans and presents the demonstration. The demonstrator should have a thorough knowledge of whatever he is to demonstrate, have a plan for the demonstration, an analysis of the job to be demonstrated, everything ready and the demonstration area arranged as he would expect the learner to do it. If the demonstration requires more than one person, all persons involved should be capable of working smoothly and accurately together (usually the demonstrator also acts as chairman and commentator).

2. *A commentator* may be used to explain the demonstration while another person(s) carries it on. If a commentator takes part in the demonstration, he should (a) thoroughly understand the procedure to be demonstrated, (b) be familiar with the exact manner in which the demonstrator conducts the procedure, and (c) have the self-discipline to refrain from allowing his com-

64

mentary to overshadow the demonstration itself since the commentary is complementary to the demonstration.

3. *The chairman* handles the arrangements for the demonstration, introduces it, and concludes it. He does not necessarily know a great deal about the procedure to be demonstrated.

4. *The learners* observe the demonstration, seek to understand it, ask necessary questions, and practice the procedure after they have seen it done.

D. *What is the usual pattern of communication?*

The oral communication flows from the demonstrator to the audience or learner. That is, the chairman (if one is used) and the demonstrator talk to the learners who listen and observe. The learners are encouraged to ask questions when the demonstration has been completed. The pattern of communication can be represented diagramatically as follows:

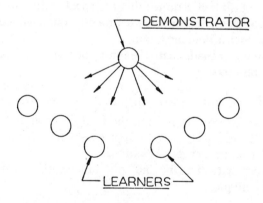

E. *What are the advantages and limitations of the demonstration?*

1. *Advantages:*

a. This technique can usually clarify a procedure better than an oral or written description of it;

b. A good demonstration has vividness, clarity, and an easily observed and understood sequence of steps and key points to be learned;

c. The learner is given an opportunity to have his proficiency tested at once by performing the procedure under the direction of the demonstrator. Errors in procedure can be corrected at once;

d. The learner has practice opportunities under expert guidance.

2. *Limitations:*

a. The equipment or properties used in the demonstration may be too bulky or immobile to bring to the meeting place, making it necessary for the audience to go to another location for the demonstration;

b. It may be difficult to arrange for all learners to imitate what they have seen demonstrated;

c. The technique is limited to teaching in practical rather than abstract areas;

d. Since adults who are not professional teachers often hesitate to take on a task that requires them to speak with authority, it is sometimes difficult to convince a properly qualified person that he can conduct a demonstration;

e. A clumsy or inadequate demonstration can lead to unfavorable audience reaction.

F. Check list for appraising the demonstration

This list can be used in making the final decision as to whether or not the demonstration is an appropriate technique to use for a particular adult learning situation.

If the replies tend to be "no" or "undecided," consider using another technique.

	Yes	No	Unde-cided
1. Are procedures involved that lend themselves to demonstration with			
a. The facilities available (appropriate room, materials, etc.)?	___	___	___
b. The expected audience?	___	___	___
c. The time available?	___	___	___
2. Is the procedure too complex to be demonstrated?	___	___	___

3. Is a qualified demonstrator available? _____ _____ _____

4. Can the necessary equipment be obtained

    a. For the demonstrator? _____ _____ _____

    b. For each audience member to try out what he has learned? _____ _____ _____

5. Are there clear-cut goals to achieve? _____ _____ _____

6. Is a chairman available who can carry out his responsibilities (if one is desired)? _____ _____ _____

7. Are there other techniques that might be more appropriate choices? _____ _____ _____

If yes, what are they and why? _____

_____

_____

G. What are the responsibilities that go with the demonstration?

1. What does the chairman do?

a. *Prior to the demonstration,* the chairman:

(1) Makes certain that he understands what is to be demonstrated and the goals of the demonstration;

(2) Tries to understand the relationship of the demonstration to other parts of the program or series;

(3) Meets with the demonstrator in order to:

(a) Get to know him,

(b) Find out whether or not the demonstrator will make his own explanation to the learners or prefer having it done by a commentator,

(c) Learn how the demonstration will be carried out and how long it will take,

(d) Find out what equipment and special properties or facilities will be necessary and who should supply them. Will the demonstrator accompany the demonstration with slides or charts? Will he want a blackboard? Should precautions be taken to insure learner safety or guard against damage to the meeting room or its furnishings?

(e) Explain to the demonstrator the need for a demonstration,

(f) Get suggestions from the demonstrator regarding ways to make the demonstration effective for the learners,

(g) Clarify any financial responsibilities that might be involved;

(4) Sees that proper physical arrangements are made so that the demonstrator will be able to function effectively and the learners will be able to *see and hear clearly at all times;*

(5) Investigates the kinds of printed materials that can be distributed to the learners before or after the demonstration;

(6) Meets with the commentator to get to know him (if a commentator is to be used to explain the demonstration). The commentator will need to know (a) the goals of the demonstration, (b) the characteristics of the learners, (c) the specific steps to be taken in the demonstration, and (d) whether questions from the learners are to be encouraged during the demonstration or after it is over;

(7) Considers the characteristics of the anticipated learners, taking into account the possible implications of their age, sex, background, and previous experience with the procedure to be demonstrated; in what respects their abilities and interests will vary; and how all learners can be motivated to take part in the demonstration with interest and the desire to learn;

(8) Prepares a brief introduction that will make clear the following:

(a) What is to be demonstrated and why,

(b) Why the process is worth learning—specifically referring to the use of this knowledge,

(c) The name, title, background, and qualifications of the demonstrator(s),

(d) The relationship of the demonstration to other parts of the program or series,

(e) When and how the learner is expected to ask questions for clarification,

(f) When the learner will have opportunities to practice what is being demonstrated,

(g) Any safety precautions that may be necessary;

b. *After the demonstration,* the chairman:

(1) Thanks the demonstrator for his presentation;

(2) Distributes reading materials for follow-up study (if appropriate);

(3) Encourages the learners to put to use what they have learned and makes suggestions for doing so;

(4) Returns the control of the meeting to the appropriate person or closes the meeting himself;

(5) Looks for opportunities after the meeting to check on the learners' progress.

2. *What does the demonstrator do?*

a. *Prior to the demonstration,* the demonstrator:

(1) Makes certain that he understands (a) the purpose of the demonstration, (b) the time available, and (c) the characteristics of the expected audience;

(2) Decides what visual aids he will use to accompany his presentation and arranges for procuring them;

(3) Prepares his demonstration by:

(a) Deciding exactly what will be covered,

(b) Developing a step-by-step plan,

(c) Running through the demonstration, synchronizing his explanation to his actions, before the meeting;

(4) Considers how the more difficult steps can be clarified by the use of visual aids, models, or repetition (Visual aids should be attractive and easily seen throughout the room.);

(5) Understands that the only purpose of the demonstration is to assist the learners to master the procedure;

(6) Brings all of his equipment to the meeting place and carefully arranges it for effective use;

b. *During the demonstration,* the demonstrator:

(1) Prepares the learners by:

(a) Putting them at ease,

(b) Finding out what they already know about the process,

(c) Arousing their interest so that they will be eager to learn the process;

(2) Presents the demonstration by:

(a) Telling, showing, and illustrating carefully and patiently,

(b) Stressing key points (points of importance which can be easily memorized),

(c) Teaching clearly and completely, emphasizing one point at a time, but no more than the learner can master,

(d) Summarizing, repeating, and questioning the learners;

(3) Asks each learner to perform by:

(a) Having him repeat the processes he saw demonstrated,

(b) Having him tell about and show the demonstrator each step in the process and repeat the key points,

(c) Asking him appropriate questions, beginning with "Why," "Who," "How," "What," "When," or "Where,"

(d) Observing his performance and correcting any errors,

(e) Repeating instructions if necessary.

3. *If a commentator is used,* he:

a. Tries to coordinate smoothly with the demonstrator;

b. Avoids overshadowing the demonstrator by too much commentary;

c. Follows the suggestions given (above) for the demonstration.

4. *What does the learner do?*

a. He prepares for the demonstration by doing any reading that may be suggested;

b. He listens and observes carefully, letting the demonstrator know when something is not clear or cannot be seen or heard;

c. He undertakes the learning steps when practice opportunities are given;

d. He continues to practice after the meeting until skill is acquired.

H. Physical arrangements and learners' comfort

1. Physical set-up.

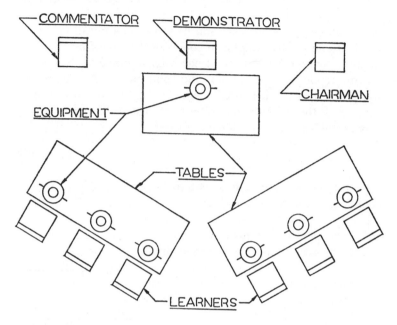

2. Learners' comfort:

a. The learners should be comfortably seated and not face a glaring light;

b. Extremes in temperature are distracting. Ask one person to be responsible for maintaining proper temperature and ventilation. The size of the group determines the extent to which the temperature can be expected to rise during the meeting;

c. Provide a platform or stage if necessary;

d. Select a room appropriate to the size of the group and the nature of the demonstration (some conference centers have special rooms for demonstrations);

e. If necessary, provide name cards for the personnel on the platform.

I. How to evaluate after the demonstration

The following check list will aid in appraising how effectively this technique has been conducted. It is for the use of (1) the persons who selected the demonstration as the appropriate technique and (2) those who see and hear the demonstration.

It is useful to have duplicate copies of this check list available for use after the demonstration has been presented.

If the replies tend to be "no" and "undecided," the demonstration probably has been used *ineffectively;* future errors can be avoided if the various replies are discussed briefly by those responsible for this educational procedure.

	Yes	No	Unde-cided
1. Did the procedure turn out to be a suitable one for demonstration?	___	___	___
2. Can the expense and the amount of time in preparation be justified?	___	___	___
3. Were safety and damage precautions taken?	___	___	___
4. Were the physical arrangements appropriate?			
a. Learners' comfort?	___	___	___
b. Vision and hearing?	___	___	___
c. Charts and graphs?	___	___	___
d. Proper equipment, neatly arranged and well organized?	___	___	___
5. Was the chairman's introduction clear and to the point?	___	___	___
6. Did the introduction make clear:			
a. The purpose of the demonstration?	___	___	___
b. Why the process is worth learning?	___	___	___
c. The relationship of the demonstration to other parts of the program or series (if such exists)?	___	___	___
7. Was the demonstration:			
a. Clear and understandable?	___	___	___
b. Given with cordiality?	___	___	___

c. Illustrated adequately? ____ ____ ____
d. Shown in a step-by-step manner? ____ ____ ____
e. Of appropriate length? ____ ____ ____
8. Were key points stressed? ____ ____ ____
9. Were questions
a. Encouraged? ____ ____ ____
b. Answered courteously? ____ ____ ____
10. If several demonstrators were used, did they work as a team? ____ ____ ____
11. Did the learners show interest? ____ ____ ____
12. Did the learners get practice opportunities? ____ ____ ____
13. Can the learners reasonably be expected to acquire skill in the procedure(s) demonstrated? ____ ____ ____
14. Was there evidence of willingness to accept responsibility for practicing the procedure demonstrated? ____ ____ ____
15. Was there evidence of learner skill when the demonstrator made his follow-up visit? ____ ____ ____

J. How the demonstration might be used— an example

The training committee for a local council of Girl Scouts is holding a series of training meetings for newly selected troop leaders. One of the purposes of these meetings is to teach the leaders certain camping procedures. Among other things, the leaders should know how to "pitch" and "strike" a tent. This can best be taught by a demonstration. The demonstrator secures the necessary equipment and moves the group of new leaders out-of-doors. The demonstration then proceeds in a step-by-step fashion until the tent is satisfactorily set up. Each learner is then given the opportunity to practice by pitching a tent provided for that purpose. Each step is carefully checked by the demonstrator. After everyone has successfully demonstrated his knowledge and skill in pitching a tent, the "striking," or disassembling and packing, is demonstrated and practiced by each person in the group.

IV. Field Trip

A. What is the field trip?

A field trip is a carefully planned educational tour in which a group visits an object or place of interest for first-hand observation and study.

The learning group makes its tour under the guidance of a person well-informed about the area under consideration. This person answers questions and points out features that might not be seen readily by the learners. The field trip should be followed by careful analysis, interpretation, or discussion of the places visited and the information obtained. A group can explore the significance of what they have observed on a field trip using other techniques such as group discussion, a panel-forum, or a speech-forum.

B. When should the field trip be used?

When you wish to accomplish one or more of the following, the field trip is appropriate:

1. To provide first-hand observation and study of something that cannot readily be brought to the learning group;

2. To stimulate interest and concern about conditions or problems that need study;

3. To illustrate the results of practice or a course of action in its natural environment;

4. To relate theoretical study to practical application.

C. Who are the personnel involved?

1. *A coordinator* sees that the necessary arrangements are made and guides the group through the trip. (If he also leads the group in interpretation and discussion of the trip, he should be skilled in discussion leadership; however, another qualified person can and frequently does accept this responsibility.) He should be a person who takes his responsibilities seriously and attends carefully to details. In addition he should be well-informed concerning the place to be visited.

2. *The guide* may or may not be used. He is a person familiar with the local conditions and characteristics of the place or object to be observed. If he is used, the coordinator turns over the direc-

tion of the trip to him upon arrival at the place to be visited. The guide then directs the group to points of interest. Upon completion of this part of the trip, he returns control of the trip to the coordinator.

A guide is used if local operating conditions require such a procedure, and only if the person who is to serve as guide can be counted upon to provide the kind of leadership that will attempt to meet the interests and goals of the participants.

3. *The participants* are all of the persons who take part in the trip. The success of the trip will depend upon the participants using it as an opportunity to learn.

D. What is the usual pattern of communication?

During the field trip the coordinator or the guide points out important features to be observed, sometimes to the entire group and sometimes to individuals. The participants are free to raise questions and to talk among themselves.

E. Advantages and limitations of the field trip

1. *Advantages:*

a. This technique makes possible direct, first-hand experience —opportunities to apply several senses to the learning venture;

b. A field trip can provide a group with a common experience that can be used as a resource for further learning activities;

c. It is usually more satisfactory to have the learner observe and study something first hand than it is to try to describe it to him;

d. The experience of observing in the company of other learners, an informed coordinator and guide can stimulate the learner to keener and more accurate observations;

e. The trip can help the learner to appreciate another point of view or open entirely new areas to him;

f. The informality that characterizes the field trip can help the learners to know each other better—a helpful step in the learning process.

2. *Limitations:*

a. A field trip depends upon the availability and accessibility of whatever is to be observed (Operating schedules or other local restrictions can stand in the way.);

b. Some persons may have physical handicaps that prevent their taking the trip;

c. The possibilities of injury are always present;

d. The learners may not be able to spend the time necessary for the trip.

F. Check list for appraising the field trip

This list can be used in making the final decision as to whether or not the field trip is an appropriate technique to use for a particular adult learning situation.

If the answers tend to be "no" or "undecided," consider using another technique.

	Yes	No	Unde-cided
1. Are we using this technique to accomplish one or more of the following:			
a. To provide opportunities for first-hand study and observation?	_____	_____	_____
b. To assist in providing a variety of learning experiences?	_____	_____	_____
c. To stimulate interest and concern about problems or conditions that need study?	_____	_____	_____
d. To illustrate the results of practice or course of action?	_____	_____	_____
e. To relate theoretical study to practical application?	_____	_____	_____
2. Do we have clear-cut goals to achieve?	_____	_____	_____
3. Does first-hand study and observation seem to be essential?	_____	_____	_____
4. Can arrangements for the trip be made so that:			
a. All interested learners can participate without too much interference with their total work schedule?	_____	_____	_____
b. Safety and comfort can be insured?	_____	_____	_____

76

c. The trip will not interfere seriously with scheduling and rules at the place to be visited?   _____ _____ _____

5. Are we reasonably assured that the group members are interested in taking this trip?   _____ _____ _____

6. Will there be time and place for interpretation and discussion of the trip after its completion?   _____ _____ _____

7. Do we have available a coordinator who can:

a. See that the necessary arrangements for travel are made?   _____ _____ _____

b. Go over the entire trip in advance?   _____ _____ _____

c. Promote careful observation on the part of the learners?   _____ _____ _____

d. See to it that the trip is a profitable learning experience?   _____ _____ _____

8. Are there other techniques that might be more appropriate choices?   _____ _____ _____

If yes, what are they and why? _____

_____

_____

G. *Responsibilities of the personnel on the field trip*

1. *What does the coordinator do?*

a. *Prior to the trip,* the coordinator:

(1) Considers the characteristics of the group involved. He considers their age, sex, background, experience, and abilities in order to assist them to have a pleasant experience and learn most effectively. What will they have in common? In what respects will their interests and backgrounds vary? What are the implications of all this for conducting the field trip?

(2) Considers what handicaps or physical disabilities might present problems or call for special arrangements;

(3) Makes all preliminary arrangements with officials of the

organization or institution to be visited. These arrangements should include:

(a) The exact arrival time,

(b) The meeting place (address) or starting point of visitation,

(c) An approximate time schedule for the entire visit,

(d) A list of the major items to be observed or studied by the visitors,

(e) An opportunity for questions and answers after completion of the physical portion of the visit,

(f) The location of food facilities;

(4) Becomes acquainted with local guide (if one is used). The coordinator carefully orients the guide concerning the nature of the group, its goals, and the particular purpose this field trip is designed to achieve;

(5) Learns about resources—brochures, maps, charts, and diagrams—that are available for use by the group. If such learning aids are necessary, he obtains them;

(6) Checks the scheduling arrangements, allowing ample time for travel;

(7) Determines how to handle questions that arise during the field trip:

(a) Are the participants to write them down for answering later?

(b) Are they to ask the coordinator or an accompanying guide?

(c) Will the tour be halted periodically or at a specific point to permit questioning and discussion?

(8) Considers reading opportunities that can be suggested to the participants as advanced preparation;

(9) Makes provision for the participants to analyze and discuss what they have observed at the conclusion of the field trip or at a later time and place. (This might be done through group discussion, a question and answer period, or other appropriate techniques and devices.)

(10) Gives these preliminary instructions (verbally or in writing) to the persons expected to participate in the trip:

(a) A summary of the nature, purpose, extent, and cost of the trip,

(b) A careful description of the travel arrangements, clothing to wear, special equipment to bring, and safety precautions to observe,

(c) Suggestions for advance study,

(d) An explanation of the way in which the group is to analyze and discuss the trip after its completion;

(11) Prepares an introduction to be delivered to the group when it assembles to take the trip. The following points can be covered in this introduction (If a guide is used, the guide may be the logical person to convey part of this information to the group.):

(a) The purpose of the trip,

(b) A reminder that the trip is designed as a learning experience and not a lark,

(c) Suggestions as to what to observe during the trip,

(d) Rules and regulations (*with particular emphasis on safety*);

b. *During the field trip,* the coordinator:

(1) Collects waivers from the participants (if necessary);

(2) Gives his introduction (see above);

(3) Introduces the group to appropriate persons at the place to be visited;

(4) Tries to make certain that everyone can see and hear clearly;

(5) Encourages careful observation;

(6) Looks out for the health and safety of the participants;

c. *After the field trip,* the coordinator:

(1) Assists the group to analyze and discuss the significance of what has been observed;

(2) Encourages appropriate study and action based on what has been learned.

2. *What does the local guide do* (if one is used)?

a. He seeks to understand the interests of the participants and the goals of this field trip;

b. He carefully coordinates his responsibilities with those of the coordinator;

c. He avoids using words that are unfamiliar to the participants or explains the meaning of unfamiliar terms;

d. He enforces local safety rules and other procedures necessary for direction of the visitors.

3. *What is expected of the participants?* The participants' responsibilities include:

a. Appropriate advanced study and preparation with emphasis on the subject to be studied and the purpose of this particular trip;

b. Observance of rules and regulations relating to safety and local operations;

c. Thoughtful observation during the trip—observation based on the goals and the kind of interpretation or discussion that is scheduled to follow the trip;

d. Requests for clarification when necessary;

e. Use of the trip as a learning experience;

f. Careful note-taking;

g. Appropriate follow-up study and action.

H. Physical conditions, comfort, and safety

1. Examine the place to be toured for possible harm or injury to the participants—provide safety instructions and warning signs if necessary;

2. Use well-qualified licensed drivers and insured transportation;

3. Consider special group insurance and waivers for the particular trip;

4. Decide if first-aid equipment should be taken on the trip;

5. Decide if loud speakers will be necessary. Portable equipment powered by batteries can often be obtained, or a megaphone can be used;

6. Make special arrangements for persons having disabilities;

7. Determine what clothing and equipment should be brought by each participant—e.g., flashlight, overshoes, overalls, raincoat, sunglasses, fieldglasses;

8. Provide maps and diagrams and printed instructions if necessary.

I. How to evaluate after the field trip has been conducted

The following check list will aid in appraising how effectively the field trip has been conducted. It is for the use of (1) those who selected the field trip as the appropriate technique and (2) those who take part in the trip.

It is useful to have duplicated copies of this check list available for use following the trip.

If the replies tend to be "no" and "undecided," the field trip probably has been used *ineffectively;* future errors can be avoided if the various replies are discussed briefly in a cooperative way.

	Yes	No	Unde-cided
1. Did whatever was observed lend itself to first-hand observation?	___	___	___
2. Was the comfort and safety of the group provided for?	___	___	___
3. Were the proper arrangements made?	___	___	___
4. Were instructions clear at all times?	___	___	___
5. Did the coordinator:			
a. Encourage advanced study?	___	___	___
b. Promote careful observation?	___	___	___
c. Insure that all could see and hear at all times?	___	___	___
d. Cover the essential points in his introduction?	___	___	___
e. Try to see to it that the trip was a learning experience?	___	___	___
f. Tell the group when and how it was to participate verbally?	___	___	___
g. Explain what might be expected in the way of notes and reports about the trip?	___	___	___
h. Make provision for analysis and discussion following the field trip?	___	___	___

6. Did the guide (*if one was used*):

a. Try to assist the group in meeting its needs and goals? ___ ___ ___

b. Relate carefully his responsibilities to those of the coordinator? ___ ___ ___

c. Explain the meaning of words that were unfamiliar to the participants? ___ ___ ___

7. Did the participants:

a. Prepare adequately for the trip? ___ ___ ___

b. Observe rules and regulations? ___ ___ ___

c. Ask for clarification when necessary? ___ ___ ___

d. Retain good humor in the face of unexpected developments? ___ ___ ___

e. Use the trip as a learning experience? ___ ___ ___

f. Take notes on what they observed? ___ ___ ___

8. What was accomplished:

a. Were worthwhile opportunities for observation presented? ___ ___ ___

b. Did the participants show evidence of acquiring useful information? ___ ___ ___

c. Did the group make progress toward its goals? ___ ___ ___

d. Have problems or needs emerged which point toward further study and action? ___ ___ ___

e. Was there evidence of willingness to accept responsibility for further study or action? ___ ___ ___

9. Was the field trip an appropriate technique for this learning situation? ___ ___ ___

What other techniques might have been effective and why? _____

_____

_____

J. How the field trip might be used—examples

1. A group of citizens (housewives, professional people, etc.) has been meeting as a discussion group. They become interested in industrial and labor problems. Some of the group members become concerned that there are persons in the group who know little about the ways in which people make their living in factories. It is suggested that this knowledge is a requirement for understanding our economic problems, our society and our fellow citizens. So the group takes a field trip to a local factory.

After the field trip, the group devotes at least one of its regular meetings to a discussion of the trip. Thus they seek to make the trip an integral part of their total learning experience rather than merely a diversion.

2. A group of apprentices need to have a broader knowledge of industry and its problems than is offered by the particular plant in which they are employed. A well-organized field trip is arranged to meet this objective.

3. A group of farmers is concerned about pasture problems. Under the guidance of an expert in this area of agriculture the group visits an area where farmers have developed a new pasture and grasslands program. The expert takes the group to the points of interest and shows them how others are overcoming the same problems.

The trip has the effects both of informing the group members and of encouraging them to do a better job.

It might well be that the farmers would attend a meeting following the field trip. At this meeting they might meet in discussion groups to talk over what they have seen and its possible applications to their farming practices. This would enable them to consolidate what they have learned and to try to accept the idea of changing their own practices.

V. Forum

A. What is a forum?

A forum is a 15- to 60-minute period of open discussion that is carried on among the members of an entire group (usually larger than 25 persons), and one or more resource persons. The forum is directed by a moderator.

The term "forum" is also used to mean any large public educational meeting in which various techniques are used and the audience participates verbally. In this book we are using the term in a more precise way and recommending that the forum be used in combination with other techniques. The techniques most often followed by a forum are the speech, the panel, and symposium (modern concept), the interview, the demonstration, and the role-play.*

It should be noted that the forum is *not* a question and answer period, but rather a guided discussion during which the audience is encouraged to make comments, raise and discuss issues, and offer information, as well as ask questions of each other and the resource person.

B. When should a forum be used?

This technique can be used when the topics and goals point toward accomplishing one or more of the following:

1. Clarifying or exploring issues raised or information presented previously by means of another technique;

2. Enabling the audience to contribute ideas and opinions;

3. Conducting a more thorough discussion than a question and answer period permits;

4. Permitting resource persons to speak to needs and interests as they emerge from discussion;

5. Identifying needs and interests to be met by further programming.

C. Who are the personnel involved?

1. *The moderator* presents an introduction and guides the discussion. He should be skilled in leading discussion and stimulating the participation in a large audience;

2. *The resource person(s)* answers questions, supplies information, offers comments and ideas for further discussion. He does

---

* A forum would not follow group discussion, colloquy, or ancient symposium because these techniques have many of the same characteristics and uses as the forum.

not give a prepared presentation; he makes brief, direct remarks. He should have sound knowledge of and interest in the topic(s) to be considered;

3. *The audience* should have enough knowledge about the topic(s) to permit intelligent discussion.

D. What is the usual pattern of communication?

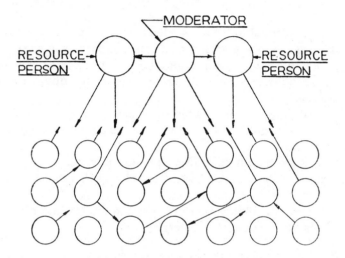

This diagram shows that the forum is discussion by a large audience. The audience members speak to each other as well as to the moderator and resource person(s).

E. What are the advantages and limitations of the forum?

1. *Advantages:*

a. Audience members have opportunities to participate verbally;

b. Resource persons usually make careful preparation when they know that they are to take part in a forum and are more likely to consider the needs and interests of the audience;

c. Audience members tend to listen actively to the presentation that precedes the forum because they know that verbal participation will be expected of them;

d. Resource persons' knowledge and the experience of the participants can be brought to bear on the needs and interests as they emerge;

e. Audience members can get clarification of points that were not made clear in the presentations that precede the forum.

2. *Limitations:*

a. It is essential to have a moderator with skill and experience in guiding discussion among members of a large audience;

b. It is difficult, with a large audience, to have enough time for each audience member to make a verbal contribution to the discussion;

c. It is difficult to encourage some persons to participate verbally in a large group because they lack the necessary information or interest; .

d. It is sometimes difficult to provide physical conditions in some auditoriums and meeting rooms which will permit adequate discussion by a large audience;

e. It requires resource persons who are flexible and can treat problems and needs as they emerge.

F. Check list for appraising the forum as a choice of technique

This list can be used in making the final decision as to whether or not the forum is an appropriate technique to use for a particular adult learning situation.

If the answers tend to be "no" and "undecided," consider using another technique.

	Yes	No	Unde-cided
1. Are we using this technique to accomplish one or more of the following:			
a. To clarify or explore information or issues raised previously by means of another technique?	_____	_____	_____

86

b. To encourage verbal participation by the audience?   _____ _____ _____

c. To permit resource persons to deal with needs and interests as they emerge from discussion?   _____ _____ _____

d. To identify needs and interests to be met by further programming?   _____ _____ _____

2. Do we have clear-cut goals to achieve?   _____ _____ _____

3. Is the topic:

a. Appropriately worded for discussion?   _____ _____ _____

b. Of interest to the audience members?   _____ _____ _____

c. Within the knowledge and range of experience of the audience members?   _____ _____ _____

4. Can we:

a. Provide a physical set-up helpful to discussion?   _____ _____ _____

b. Insure audience comfort?   _____ _____ _____

5. Is a moderator available to:

a. Instruct the resource person(s)?   _____ _____ _____

b. Understand and show interest in the topic?   _____ _____ _____

c. Provide a satisfactory introduction?   _____ _____ _____

d. Plan for and encourage participation by all?   _____ _____ _____

e. Keep the discussion moving?   _____ _____ _____

f. Prevent the resource person(s) from excessively dominating discussion?   _____ _____ _____

g. Properly use the forum as a technique?   _____ _____ _____

6. Are there resource persons available who:

a. Can work informally and flexibly?   _____ _____ _____

b. Can stay on the topic?   _____ _____ _____

c. Can refrain from excessively dominating?   _____ _____ _____

d. Are not afraid to say, "I don't know" during discussion?   _____ _____ _____

e. Have sound knowledge of the topic?   _____ _____ _____

f. Will use language that the audience understands?   _____ _____ _____

g. Will try to understand and work toward the goals?   _____ _____ _____

7. Will the audience have sufficient information about the topic to discuss it thoughtfully?   _____ _____ _____

8. Are there other techniques that might be more appropriate?   _____ _____ _____

If yes, what are they and why? _____

_____

_____

G. Responsibilities of the personnel involved in a forum

1. *What does the moderator do?*

a. *Prior to the forum,* the moderator:

(1) Keeps in mind the topics to be covered and the goals sought, developing some questions appropriate for discussion;

(2) Tries to understand how the forum works;

(3) Explains to the resource person(s) how the forum will function;

(4) Gets to know the resource person(s) so that he can introduce them and assist the group to make the best possible use of the knowledge each resource person has;

(5) Plans for physical arrangements that will be conducive to discussion and audience comfort;

(6) Studies the characteristics of the group that is anticipated: the age, sex, background, and attitudes of the expected audience members, what they will have in common, the ways in which their interest and knowledge of the topic(s) will vary—considering the implications of all this for conducting the forum, especially for encouraging participation;

(7) Prepares a short introduction to use in opening the forum. The introduction will make clear:

(a) The topic—why it is important and worth discussing,

(b) The goals of the session, and the series as a whole,

(c) The amount of time available for the forum,

(d) The nature of the forum (how it works) and its relationship to the technique which precedes it,

(e) The responsibilities of the audience and the resource persons,

(f) The various ways in which audience members can contribute to discussion,

(g) The necessary background information: definitions, statistics, and other facts,

(h) The names, background, and qualifications of the resource persons;

b. *During the forum,* the moderator:

(1) Presents his introduction (see above);

(2) Begins the discussion by offering a question for discussion;

(3) Improvises questions when they seem appropriate;

(4) Keeps the discussion from bogging down on one question or issue;

(5) Encourages the sharing of ideas and opinions in a friendly atmosphere;

(6) Makes such summaries as seem necessary in the course of the discussion and in closing;

(7) Keeps in mind the goals to be met and the topics to be covered by discussion;

(8) Makes certain that every person hears every word spoken —restating contributions when necessary;

(9) Prohibits a monopoly of talk by one person or a few by:

(a) Warning the group of this danger in his introduction,

(b) Calling on persons who wish to contribute,

(c) Politely but firmly cutting short those contributions that tend to be overly long or rambling;

(10) Suggests follow-up study to the audience.

Encouraging thoughtful participation by everyone who wishes to speak may be the major problem facing the moderator. When groups are large (over 50 persons) it is difficult to overcome fear and timidity which inhibit participation. The good moderator anticipates this difficulty and tries to overcome it in several ways:

(a) He has studied the characteristics of the group expected to be present;

(b) He has identified aspects of the topic(s) that tend to interest as many persons as possible;

(c) He has developed some provocative questions;

(d) He has provided the best physical arrangements possible;

(e) He tactfully controls participants who speak too long or outside the subject under consideration.

2. *What do the resource persons do?*

a. *Prior to the forum,* the resource persons:

(1) Familiarize themselves with the mechanics of the technique to be used (forum);

(2) Study the characteristics of the audience expected to be present;

(3) Try to understand the relationship of their part of the program to the total program;

(4) Familiarize themselves with the goals of the forum;

(5) Prepare to participate flexibly and informally;

b. *During the forum,* the resource persons:

(1) Try to avoid being forced into a dominating role;

(2) Make brief, direct comments;

(3) Encourage those present to use them (the resource persons) as resources—in much the same way that one uses a reference book;

(4) Deal constructively with needs, problems, and interests as they emerge from discussion;

(5) Use words that the audience members understand;

(6) Say "I don't know" when a question is outside their area of knowledge, or refer the participant to a source for his answer.

3. *What does the audience do?*

a. *Prior to the forum,* the audience members:

(1) Study, think, and talk about the topic(s) to be discussed;

(2) Seek to understand their responsibilities in a forum;

b. *During the forum,* the audience members:

(1) Listen actively and participate verbally by:
(a) Asking questions,
(b) Offering information,
(c) Requesting clarification,
(d) Giving examples from their personal experience,
(e) Helping to clarify for others;
(2) Help prevent a monopoly of talk by one person or a few;
(3) Insist politely but firmly that the moderator and the resource persons deal with the concerns of the audience;
(4) Help prevent turning the discussion into a debate;
(5) Undertake whatever follow-up study and action are appropriate.

H. Physical arrangements and audience comfort

1. Physical set-up.

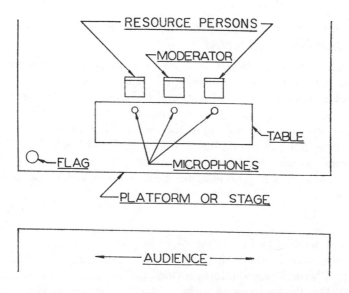

2. *Audience comfort.* Keep the following in mind when making arrangements:

a. Extremes in temperature are distracting;

b. All persons involved should be comfortably seated. No one should face a glaring light;

c. All persons should be in a face-to-face arrangement so as to permit optimum discussion. With a very large group the best that can be done in this respect is usually to arrange chairs in concentric semicircles (as is shown in "the pattern of communication," p. 44);

d. Select a room or auditorium appropriate to the size of the group;

e. Provide a platform or stage if necessary;

f. Provide a public address system if necessary (With a very large audience, microphones for audience use will be almost essential. Be sure to check carefully in advance the operation of the public address system.);

g. A blackboard or easel will usually be needed to keep topics and discussion questions before the group;

h. Provide large name cards to identify the moderator and resource person(s).

I. How to evaluate after the forum has been conducted

The following check list will aid in appraising how effectively this technique has been conducted. It is for the use of (1) the persons who selected the forum and (2) those who take part in it.

It is useful to have mimeographed or dittoed copies of the check list available for use at the end of the forum.

If the trend of the replies is toward "no" and "undecided," the forum probably has been used *ineffectively;* future errors can be avoided if the various replies are discussed briefly in a cooperative way.

	Yes	No	Unde-cided
1. Was the physical arrangement helpful to discussion by the audience?	___	___	___
2. Was audience comfort provided for?	___	___	___
3. Did the topic prove to be:			
a. Appropriately worded?	___	___	___
b. Of interest to all?	___	___	___
c. Within the knowledge and experience of the audience?	___	___	___

4. Did the moderator:

a. Instruct the resource persons carefully? _____ _____ _____

b. Provide a satisfactory introduction? _____ _____ _____

c. Guide the discussion effectively? _____ _____ _____

d. Encourage all persons to participate? _____ _____ _____

e. Point out the goals to be achieved? _____ _____ _____

5. Did the resource person(s):

a. Stay on the topic? _____ _____ _____

b. Supply only such information as was requested? _____ _____ _____

c. Encourage discussion and differing points of view? _____ _____ _____

6. Did the audience members participate effectively? _____ _____ _____

7. Did the audience members have enough knowledge to participate effectively? _____ _____ _____

8. What was accomplished?

a. Were worthwhile points made in the discussion? _____ _____ _____

b. Did members of the audience show evidence of having acquired information, new viewpoints, or of having changed attitudes? _____ _____ _____

c. Did the group make progress toward their goal(s)? _____ _____ _____

d. Did problems or needs emerge which pointed toward further study or action? _____ _____ _____

e. Was there evidence of willingness to accept responsibility for further study or action? _____ _____ _____

9. Was the forum an appropriate technique for this learning situation? _____ _____ _____

What other techniques might have been effective and why? _____

_____

_____

J. How the forum might be used—an example

A neighborhood has been plagued by vandalism and irresponsible behavior by teenagers. A group of citizens is planning a meeting to confront the problem. They expect an audience of about 50 persons. A symposium will be used to explain some of the causes of delinquency and what other neighborhoods have done to develop constructive activities for teenagers. The speakers will be a psychologist, a social worker, a clergyman, and a teacher. The planning committee wants to follow the symposium with a technique that will enable the audience to carry on a productive discussion of the implications of what has been said about the causes of delinquency. That is, they wish for the entire group to discuss "What Can Our Neighborhood Do About This Problem of Vandalism?" The planning committee considers using group discussion (dividing the audience into three discussion groups, each of which would discuss the topic just mentioned). They reject this technique because:

1. Their meeting place does not have three rooms that are well-suited for group discussion;

2. A sufficient number of *trained* discussion leaders is not available;

3. They wish to have all the speakers available as resource persons when the topic is discussed by the audience.

The committee eventually elects to follow the symposium with a forum for these reasons:

1. They have available a well-qualified moderator;

2. The speakers can serve as resource persons for the forum;

3. The entire audience can discuss the topic together. This is desirable because it is the entire neighborhood that is eventually going to have to take action;

4. The topic is suitable for discussion by a relatively large group.

VI. GROUP DISCUSSION

A. What is group discussion?

Group discussion is purposeful conversation and deliberation about a topic of mutual interest among six to 20 participants under the guidance of a trained participant called a leader.

Group discussion is a technique that offers maximum opportunity for the individual learner to share his ideas and experiences with others. If people fail to accept their responsibilities or are untrained in this technique, enlightened conversation will give way to debate, argument, or a pooling of ignorance. *The entire group should have training in the fundamentals of participation of which leadership is a part.*

It is important that the group discuss topics that lend themselves to the discussion technique. A good discussion topic meets the following criteria:

1. It interests participants in the group;
2. It is possible for the participants to have, or acquire, enough information to discuss it meaningfully;
3. It is clearly worded and understood;
4. It might suggest different points of view.

B. When should group discussion be used?

This educational technique can be used for one or more of the following purposes:

1. To encourage people to become aware of and learn about problems of their neighborhood, community, institution, or organization;
2. To enable the participant to express his opinions in a group;
3. To learn about topics of mutual interest;
4. To develop a nucleus of persons for intelligent leadership in a neighborhood, institution, or organization;
5. To learn about relationships necessary to mature living;
6. To identify, explore, or solve a problem;
7. To decide on a plan of action.

C. Who are the personnel involved?

1. *The leader* is the person who guides the discussion. He is not necessarily an expert in the subject or problem area from which the topic comes. He needs (or should be willing to acquire) enough knowledge to understand the significance of the topic and the issue that it suggests. It is important to remember that leadership is a role that a trained participant temporarily accepts. It is not a position that is permanently bestowed on someone. Most discussion groups rotate leadership in order to develop a broad base of competent leadership and provide as many persons as possible with insight into the problems and duties of the leader.

Using two leaders. Often two person guide a discussion, one termed the leader and the other the co-leader. The co-leader assists the leader in any way that seems appropriate in planning and conducting the discussion. He helps develop suggested purposes, an outline, and discussion questions. He may record the significant contributions made during the discussion on a blackboard or easel.

2. *The group participants* are those persons who take an active part in the discussion. They presumably are (a) interested in the topic, (b) willing to prepare for the discussion, and (c) willing to accept responsibility for sharing their ideas and opinions.

3. *The recorder* writes on paper such information as the group feels will be useful to record. He may be requested to record such matters as the points of agreement or disagreement, suggested action, or recommendations. He may copy what is written on the blackboard or easel so that the blackboard can be erased from time to time.

4. A *resource person* may be used by the group during discussion in much the same way that a reference book is used. The participants request from him whatever information seems essential to meaningful discussion.

5. *An observer* may be used to watch the process. He keeps appropriate notes and, when asked, shares these reactions with the participants for the purpose of improving the discussion and interpersonal relationships. He sits away from the group where he sees what is going on, but he does not participate in the discussion.

6. *The participants* are all the persons involved in the discussion: leader, group participants, observer, recorder, and resource person.

D. What is the usual pattern of communication?

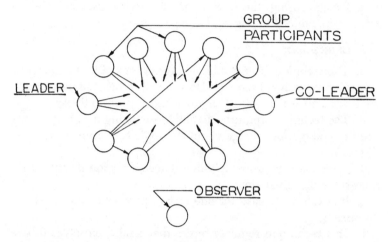

As the diagram shows, the group participants speak to one another and to the leader. The leader should not speak as frequently as the group participants; but the frequency with which the leader speaks will depend on the extent to which the group participants accept their responsibilities for the discussion. It should be kept in mind (1) that group discussion is purposeful conversation and that in no way does it resemble a series of short speeches, and (2) that much of the conversation should *not* be routed through the leader.

E. Advantages and limitations of group discussion

1. *Advantages:*

a. This technique provides those who use it with maximum opportunity for the acceptance of personal responsibility for learning;

b. A person can share his experience and opinions with others and get their reaction;

c. One can gain insight into his own behavior;

d. This technique encourages a person to develop his abilities to work as a member of a team;

e. This technique can assist a person to develop self-confidence in group situations;

f. Persons using this technique effectively usually establish friendship, understanding, and acceptance.

2. *Limitations:*

a. The technique is suitable only for groups of 6 to 20 persons;

b. Unproductive discussion often results when the participants have not had training in their roles and responsibilities;

c. The technique requires that all those taking part have or can acquire enough knowledge about the topic to permit meaningful discussion;

d. Some persons probably will not accept responsibility for the success of the discussion;

e. It is relatively easy for one or two persons to dominate the discussion;

f. This technique requires topics that lend themselves to discussion.

F. Check list for appraising group discussion

This list can be used in making the final decision as to whether or not the group discussion is an appropriate technique to use for a particular adult learning situation.

If the answers tend to be "no" or "undecided," consider using another technique.

	Yes	No	Unde-cided
1. Does the topic lend itself to discussion?	___	___	___
2. Can the topic be worded to encourage thoughtful, cooperative discussion?	___	___	___
3. Is there a clear-cut purpose for the discussion?	___	___	___
4. Is qualified leadership available?	___	___	___

5. Will the group be of appropriate size (6 to 20 persons)? _____ _____ _____

6. Will the participants have some understanding of their responsibilities? _____ _____ _____

7. Can the participants be given training in their roles and responsibilities (if needed)? _____ _____ _____

8. Are there available the necessary written materials (or a resource person) to insure that discussion is carried on in the light of authoritative information? _____ _____ _____

9. Can the necessary physical set-up be provided:

   a. Face-to-face seating? _____ _____ _____

   b. Blackboard or easel? _____ _____ _____

   c. Freedom from noises and distractions? _____ _____ _____

10. Are there other techniques that might be more appropriate? _____ _____ _____

If yes, what are they and why? _____

_____

_____

G. Responsibilities of the personnel involved in group discussion

1. *What does the leader do?*

a. *Prior to the discussion,* the leader:

(1) Reads information on the topic to be discussed and

(a) Lists the main ideas on paper,

(b) Becomes informed about any controversial issues involved;

(2) Prepares tentative purposes and a brief outline that contains three or four main points for discussion;

(3) Prepares questions to start the discussion and keeps the group moving toward their goal;

(4) Makes certain that the necessary physical arrangements can be made and that the facilities for the comfort of the group will be adequate;

(5) Plans for group participation by:

(a) Preparing to explain or review the responsibilities of the participants,

(b) Studying the characteristics of the group that is anticipated—their age, sex, background, and points of view—in order to stimulate their interest and make use of their experience,

(c) Trying to foresee the obstacles to effective participation that may arise,

(d) Encouraging the participants to do advanced study of appropriate written materials;

(6) Prepares an introduction which will

(a) Present briefly and logically the topic to be discussed,

(b) Introduce the topic by using maps, films, pictures, and other visual aids if appropriate,

(c) Explain why the topic is important, relating it to the experience and concerns of the participants,

(d) State the purpose of the discussion as the leader understands it,

(e) Encourage effective participation by all,

(f) Present a brief outline for discussion—two to four major phases that suggest themselves to the leader;

b. *Immediately before and during the discussion,* the leader

(1) Arrives early and makes the necessary physical arrangements;

(2) Welcomes the participants as they arrive, introducing himself;

(3) Sees that everyone participating is acquainted, using name cards if necessary;

(4) Writes the topic and tentative outline on blackboard or easel;

(5) Presents the introduction he has prepared (see #6 above);

(6) Suggests the purpose and the tentative outline to the group participants *for their approval or modification;*

(7) Guides the discussion, being careful not to be too aggressive or so retiring that chaos will result;

(8) Remains flexible despite the outline;

(9) Refrains from taking sides;

100

(10) Is sensitive to the needs of individual participants and the group as a whole;

(11) Encourages a productive, informal conversation shared in by all persons present;

(12) Encourages and assists the group to evaluate and try to improve its performance.

2. *What do the participants do?* They

a. Prepare for discussion by reading and thinking about the topic;

b. Share their ideas and experiences;

c. Help one another to participate effectively;

d. Listen thoughtfully;

e. Face conflict (should it arise) frankly and with understanding;

f. Ask for clarification when necessary;

g. Share responsibility for making the discussion productive;

h. Keep a minority view before the group, if one exists;

i. Refrain from carrying on "private" conversations (that is, talk between two persons who ignore the other persons present);

j. Seek to promote understanding—rather than to force acceptance of their own points of view;

k. Suggest

(1) Changes in the wording of the topic,

(2) Additions or corrections of the items in the outline suggested by the leader,

(3) Modifications or additions to the purpose of the discussion as suggested by the leader,

(4) Improvements in the physical arrangements,

(5) Opportunities and topics for future discussions,

l. Do whatever follow-up study and action that seems appropriate.

H. *Physical arrangements and group comfort*

1. *Physical set-up.*

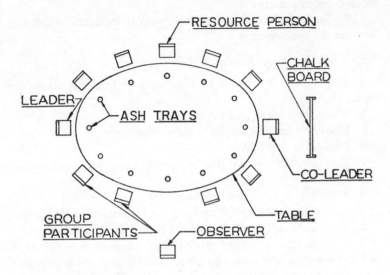

2. *Group comfort.*

a. Extremes in temperature are distracting;

b. The group must be comfortably seated in movable chairs around a table or tables;

c. The members of the group must be able to see and hear the leader and each other (face-to-face seating is essential);

d. No person should face a glaring light;

e. Select a room appropriate to the size of group, free from noise and distraction;

f. Provide a blackboard, chalk, and eraser. An easel and paper with a large black crayon is equally useful;

g. Provide crayon and a 5 × 8 card on which each person can print his name in large letters.

I. *How to evaluate after group discussion has been conducted*

The following check list should aid in appraising how effectively group discussion has been carried on. It can be used by (1) **the** persons who selected this technique and (2) those who take part in the group discussion. You may wish to have mimeographed or dittoed copies of this check list for use in evaluating the discussion.

If the replies tend to be "no" and "undecided," group discussion may well have been used ineffectively. Future mistakes can be avoided if the reasons for the various answers are discussed briefly in a cooperative spirit.

	Yes	No	Unde-cided
1. Were the following properly oriented and instructed *prior to the meeting:*			
a. The leader (or leaders)?	___	___	___
b. The participants?	___	___	___
c. The recorder (if one was used)?	___	___	___
d. The resource person (if one was used)?	___	___	___
e. The observer (if one was used)?	___	___	___
2. Was the physical set-up adequate for this technique?	___	___	___
3. Was the topic			
a. Of interest to all participants?	___	___	___
b. Appropriately phrased for discussion?	___	___	___
c. Within the knowledge and experience of the participants?	___	___	___
4. Did the leader show evidence of having			
a. Planned to encourage participation?	___	___	___
b. Carefully studied the characteristics of the group as a whole?	___	___	___
c. Encouraged the participants to do advanced study?	___	___	___
d. Stated the purpose of the discussion as he understood it?	___	___	___
e. Informed all participants of their opportunities and responsibilities?	___	___	___
f. Suggested an outline to the group?	___	___	___
g. Guided the discussion effectively?	___	___	___

h. Tried to minimize the limitations of this technique? ____ ____ ____

i. Made occasional summaries that represented group views? ____ ____ ____

j. Remained neutral? ____ ____ ____

5. If two leaders were used, did they work well together? ____ ____ ____

6. Did the participants show evidence of having understood their responsibilities:

a. Had they prepared to participate? ____ ____ ____

b. Did they listen attentively? ____ ____ ____

c. Did they contribute to the discussion? ____ ____ ____

d. Was verbal participation fairly well-balanced? ____ ____ ____

e. Did they support one another? ____ ____ ____

f. Did they face conflict frankly (if it arose)? ____ ____ ____

g. Did they permit and encourage difference of opinion, keeping minority views before the group? ____ ____ ____

h. Did they try to differentiate fact from opinion? ____ ____ ____

i. Did they ask for clarification when necessary? ____ ____ ____

j. Did they voluntarily suggest ways to improve the discussion? ____ ____ ____

7. Was effective use made of the recorder? ____ ____ ____

8. Was effective use made of the resource person? ____ ____ ____

9. What was accomplished:

a. Were worthwhile points made in the discussion? ____ ____ ____

b. Did the participants show evidence of having acquired information, new viewpoints, or of having changed attitudes? ____ ____ ____

c. Have problems or needs emerged which point toward further study or action? ____ ____ ____

104

d. Was there evidence of willingness to accept responsibility for further study or action? _____ _____ _____

10. Was group discussion an appropriate technique for this learning situation? _____ _____ _____

What other techniques might have been effective and why? _____

_____

_____

J. How group discussion might be used—an example

A series of six programs about city planning and slum clearance are to be televised over the local TV station in a city of 200,000 persons. The local adult education council sees this as an opportunity to supplement the telecasts with group learning activities. It appoints a committee to explore this possibility. Members of the committee are a librarian, a public school adult educator, and a representative of the League of Women Voters, the director of the TV series, a member of the City Planning Commission, and a member of the Urban Renewal League.

The committee explores several kinds of learning activities which might be held in conjunction with the six telecasts. These include articles in the press, special study assignments in the schools, and exhibits in libraries and store windows. They also consider holding meetings at various places throughout the community. They have difficulty clarifying the specific goals for such meetings. Are they to supplement the information presented over TV, or are they to serve as means of getting discussion and action concerning the problems presented over TV? After a time, it becomes clear that the eventual goal should be intelligent action toward solution of city planning and slum clearance problems. This will require confining the TV programs to the presenting of information and the raising of issues while leaving the discussion of problems and issues to neighborhood discussion groups. Each week the person taking part in this educational program will watch the program (which will be televised twice to insure that he can see it). Then he will meet as a member of a neighborhood discussion group to discuss the ideas and issues presented in the TV program.

The neighborhood discussion groups are scheduled for such appropriate places as libraries and schools. In neighborhoods where people are reluctant to come to these settings, churches, private homes, and even firehouses can be used. Let us assume that some well-trained discussion leaders are available from the League of Women Voters and other member organizations of the adult education council. To develop additional qualified leaders a training institute may be held. Persons scheduled to lead discussion groups are given specific information and training about ways to train their groups.

By using group discussion in this fashion the planning committee has

1. Taken into account the need for the learners to become actively involved in the learning process;
2. Taken advantage of the trained leadership available in the community;
3. Utilized the television broadcast as the authoritative resource material that is necessary if people are to discuss profitably;
4. Taken into account the fact that group discussion functions best with trained leaders and trained participants;
5. Remembered the importance of helpful physical arrangements for group discussion and appropriate facilities if all people in the community are to feel free to participate.

VII. Interview

A. What is an interview?

The interview is a 5 to 30 minute presentation conducted before an audience in which one or two resource persons respond to systematic questioning by an interviewer about a previously determined topic.

The interviewer asks the resource person(s) questions designed to explore various aspects of the topic and improvises questions as the interview progresses. The resource person has been informed in advance about the kind of questions he will be asked, but no rehearsal of the interview has been held.

The questioning is done by a member of the planning committee or a person chosen by it. Using one of the group members as interviewer usually insures that the questions asked of the resource person will be helpful to the audience members. It has the effect of bringing the audience members closer to the resource person if they identify with the interviewer.

B. When should the interview be used?

This technique can be used in adult learning situations to do the following:

1. To present information in a relaxed and informal manner;
2. To explore or analyze a problem;
3. To clarify issues;
4. To stimulate interest in a topic;
5. To encourage audience participation in a technique that is to follow the interview (for example, a forum);
6. To provide, by way of the interviewer, a bridge between the resource person(s) and the audience;
7. To obtain the impressions of an authority about an experience which he and the audience have in common; for example, when experts in adult education procedures are interviewed to evaluate a conference or workshop at its close.

C. Who are the personnel involved?

1. *The resource person* is the person who is interviewed.* Some desirable characteristics and qualifications for the resource person are:

a. Knowledge of the topic to be considered;
b. The ability to give brief, direct answers to the questions asked;
c. The ability to respond in an informal manner.

2. *The interviewer* is the person who conducts the interview. He should be interested in the topic, intellectually flexible, and resourceful. A sense of humor is also helpful. Much of the success of the interview as a learning experience will depend on his

---

* When the interview is used as a guidance and counseling technique, the person interviewed is usually termed the *interviewee*. However, *resource person* is a preferable term in the context of adult learning.

ability to ask questions which will help in exploring the topics and achieving the goals of the group. He should have enough knowledge and background about the topic to enable him to guide the interview.

3. *The audience,* the persons watching and listening, will need guidance if they are to utilize the interview as a learning experience. They may associate an interview with amusement and sit back to be entertained.

D. *What is the usual pattern of communication?*

During the interview, the talking is done by the interviewer and the resource person. The interviewer speaks directly to the audience during his introduction and his concluding remarks. During the interview, the interviewer and the resource person try to speak in such a way as to cause the audience to feel that they are a part of the conversation.

The diagram below attempts to show that the resource person and the interviewer talk to one another, while keeping in mind that their conversation is to be heard by the audience. It also shows that the interviewer occasionally speaks directly to the audience, but that the audience does not participate verbally.

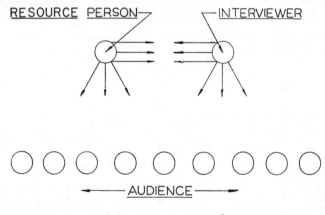

E. *Advantages and limitations of the interview*

1. *Advantages:*

a. Many resource persons prefer being interviewed to delivering a speech;

108

b. The resource person can be asked to clarify, expand, or give examples where lack of understanding seems apparent;

c. It is relatively easy to create more audience interest in the subject being treated;

d. The interview is not a complex technique.

2. *Limitations:*

a. Despite the systematic questioning that takes place, this technique does not permit a detailed presentation of information;

b. The interviewer may fail to keep the audience in mind as he plans and conducts the interview;

c. The presentation may be ineffective if the interviewer doesn't modify and supplement his prepared questions while the interview is in progress;

d. The interview may become a series of speeches if the resource person fails to give relatively short and direct answers to the questions asked.

F. Check list for appraising the interview as a choice of technique

This list can be used as a help in deciding whether or not the interview is an appropriate technique to use for a particular adult learning situation. If the answers tend to be "no" and "undecided," consider using another technique.

	Yes	No	Unde-cided
1. Are we using this technique to accomplish one or more of the following:			
a. Present information in a relaxed and informal manner?	——	——	——
b. Explore or clarify problems and issues through questioning?	——	——	——
c. Stimulate interest in the topic?	——	——	——
d. Encourage audience participation in another technique that is to follow?	——	——	——
e. Provide a bridge between the audience and the resource person?	——	——	——

f. Allow an authority to give his impression of an experience that he and the audience have in common? _____ _____ _____

2. Are we reasonably certain that verbal participation by the audience will not be essential at this point? (If it is, the use of another technique is preferable.) _____ _____ _____

3. Do we have clear-cut goals to achieve? _____ _____ _____

4. Can we:

a. Provide the proper physical set-up? _____ _____ _____

b. Insure audience comfort? _____ _____ _____

5. Do we have available an interviewer who meets these requirements:

a. Does he have some knowledge of the topic? _____ _____ _____

b. Is he interested in the topic? _____ _____ _____

c. Is he flexible and resourceful? _____ _____ _____

d. Does he have a sense of humor? _____ _____ _____

e. Can he project his voice to an audience? _____ _____ _____

f. Can he instruct the resource person about his responsibilities? _____ _____ _____

g. Can he promote thoughtful listening? _____ _____ _____

6. Do we have available a resource person who will:

a. Agree to the interview technique? _____ _____ _____

b. Answer questions concisely? _____ _____ _____

c. Refuse to answer questions that are beyond his knowledge? _____ _____ _____

d. Stay on the topic? _____ _____ _____

e. Use words the audience understands? _____ _____ _____

f. Promote learning on the part of the audience? _____ _____ _____

7. Are there other techniques that might be more appropriate? _____ _____ _____

If yes, what are they and why? _____

_____

_____

G. Responsibilities of the personnel involved in the interview

1. What does the interviewer do?

a. *Prior to the meeting,* the interviewer:

(1) Seeks to understand the goals which the interview is supposed to achieve as well as the relationships between the interview he is to conduct and the meeting as a whole (or the series of meetings, if this is the case),

(2) Develops a list of stimulating questions which will explore the topics under consideration and achieve the intended goals,

(3) Studies the characteristics of the anticipated audience. He considers their number, age, sex, knowledge of the topic, and motivations in order to help them to learn. He constantly looks for ways to make the learning experience interesting and challenging,

(4) Meets with the resource person to:

(a) Inform him about the questions to be asked, goals, and the characteristics of the expected audience,

(b) Get to know him,

(c) Test the appropriateness of the questions to be asked in the interview,

(d) Make certain that the resource person understands his responsibilities;

(5) Makes preparations to insure that the physical arrangements will promote understanding,

(6) Prepares the introduction with which he will begin the interview. The introduction will help to explain the topic; the goals and their importance; the technique to be used; the responsibilities of the audience; the length of the interview; the background and qualifications of the resource person. He should relate the topic to the experiences of the audience members if possible.

b. *During the interview,* the interviewer:

(1) Presents his introduction (see above);

(2) Conducts the interview in a conversational manner by:

(a) Putting his prepared questions to the resource person(s),

(b) Improvising questions as they seem appropriate,

(c) Clarifying or requesting clarification of remarks made by the resource persons;

(3) Asks clear, interesting questions, keeping the audience in mind at all times;

(4) Attempts to allow an appropriate amount of time for each question;

(5) Makes an occasional summary to promote understanding, if needed, and a final summary if the interview has been more than 15 minutes in length;

(6) Helps the audience to feel itself a part of the interview;

(7) Makes closing remarks which:

(a) Thank the resource person and the audience,

(b) Summarize (if he feels that a summary is needed),

(c) Encourage whatever further study and action are appropriate.

2. *What does the resource person do?*

a. *Prior to the meeting,* the resource person:

(1) Meets with the interviewer:

(a) For instructions regarding topic, goals, and the characteristics of the expected audience,

(b) To get to know him,

(c) To gain understanding of the kind of questions the interviewer intends to ask,

(d) To have his responsibilities explained;

(2) Considers the characteristics of the expected audience in order to assist them to learn;

(3) Tries to understand the interview as a technique for adult learning;

b. *During the interview,* the resource person:

(1) Answers the interviewer's questions as clearly and concisely as he can;

(2) Avoids making speeches;

(3) Tries to understand the intent of each question, asking for clarification when necessary;

(4) Says, "I don't know," when necessary;

(5) Avoids using the interview as an opportunity to display his knowledge or advance his pet theories;

(6) Uses language the audience understands.

3. *What is expected of the audience?*

a. They should be willing to undertake any advance study or preparation that is appropriate;

b. They should arrive on time and listen thoughtfully and respectfully to the interview. If the interview is to be followed by a forum or a question and answer period, then the audience member will want to note questions or comments that he wishes to bring out;

c. After the interview, the audience should be willing to undertake appropriate follow-up study and action.

H. *Physical arrangements and audience comfort*

1. *Physical set-up.*

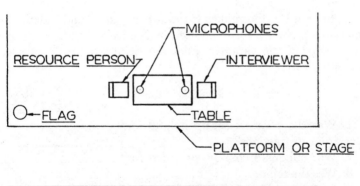

2. *Audience comfort.* Keep the following points in mind when making arrangements:

a. Participants should be comfortably seated and not face a glaring light;

b. Extremes in temperature are distracting;

c. Select a room appropriate to the size of the group;

d. Participants must be able to see and hear well. Use platform, microphones, and public address system if necessary. Be sure to test in advance the electrical outlet and the functioning of the microphones;

e. Provide drinking water for the interviewer and the resource person;

f. Provide large name cards to identify the interviewer and resource person.

I. How to evaluate after the interview has been conducted

The following check list will aid in appraising how effectively this technique has been conducted. It is for the use of (1) the persons who selected the interview as the technique to be used and (2) those who take part in it.

It may be useful to have mimeographed or dittoed copies of the check list available for use after the interview has been conducted.

If the trend of the replies is toward "no" and "undecided," the interview probably has been used ineffectively; future errors can be avoided if the various replies are discussed briefly in a co-operative way.

	Yes	No	Unde-cided
1. Was the physical set-up helpful and free from distractions?	___	___	___
2. Was adequate comfort provided for?	___	___	___
3. Was the topic:			
a. Of interest to the audience?	___	___	___
b. Appropriate in scope?	___	___	___
c. Well-worded?	___	___	___
d. Visible to the audience?	___	___	___
4. Did the interviewer:			
a. Instruct the resource person well?	___	___	___
b. Provide a satisfactory introduction?	___	___	___
c. Ask helpful questions?	___	___	___

d. Promote thoughtful listening? ____ ____ ____

e. Maintain a friendly climate? ____ ____ ____

f. Direct the interview toward the goals? ____ ____ ____

g. Make appropriate concluding remarks? ____ ____ ____

5. Did the resource person:

a. Answer questions concisely? ____ ____ ____

b. Avoid making speeches? ____ ____ ____

c. Answer questions that were not within his knowledge with "I don't know"? ____ ____ ____

d. Stay on the topic? ____ ____ ____

e. Use words the audience understood? ____ ____ ____

f. Promote learning on the part of the audience? ____ ____ ____

6. Did the audience members carry out their responsibilities? ____ ____ ____

7. What was accomplished:

a. Were worthwhile points made in the interview? ____ ____ ____

b. Did members of the audience show evidence of having acquired information, new viewpoints, or of having changed attitudes? ____ ____ ____

c. Did the group make progress toward their goals? ____ ____ ____

d. Have problems or needs emerged which point toward further study or action? ____ ____ ____

e. Was there evidence of willingness to accept responsibility for further study or action? ____ ____ ____

8. Was the interview an appropriate technique for this learning situation? ____ ____ ____

What other techniques might have been effective and why?

_____

_____

J. How the interview might be used—an example

A men's club regularly has a half-hour educational program during its weekly meeting. It is the custom to have a series of programs dealing with legislative issues several months before the state legislature convenes. The planning committee has reserved one meeting for the state legislator from its local district. The committee does not merely turn over the half-hour period to the guest, but rather discusses how to insure that the half-hour is a productive one for the membership. After considering the use of several techniques, the committee decides to use the interview, for these reasons:

1. This particular resource person has difficulty in making a brief, well-organized speech;

2. A well-qualified interviewer is available in the person of one of the club members—a teacher of political science;

3. The interview can be organized in such a way as to bring out different points of view toward pending legislation. If he were making a speech, the resource person (being a state legislator) might present only such aspects of the legislative problems that seemed favorable to his party or his personal views;

4. The interviewer can pace the interview in such a way that a maximum number of important points are considered in the short time available (30 minutes).

Prior to conducting the interview, the interviewer consults with various club members to find out what problems interest them. This consultation enables him to develop interest in the meeting. It also helps insure that the program will satisfy the expressed interests of the club members.

VIII. PANEL

A. What is the panel?

The panel is a group of three to six persons having a purposeful conversation on an assigned topic.

The panel members are selected on the basis of previously demonstrated interest and competency in the subject to be discussed and their ability to verbalize in front of an audience. The

116

panel members are usually seated at a table in front of the audience.

The conversation among the panel members is guided by a moderator who has prepared questions to start and sustain the discussion. The audience watches and listens but does not participate verbally. (Frequently the panel is followed by a forum, which does allow verbal participation by the audience.) A panel usually lasts from 15-45 minutes.

B. When should the panel be used?

The panel may be the technique to use when topics and goals point toward accomplishing one or more of the following:

1. Identifying and clarifying problems or issues;
2. Bringing several points of view before the audience;
3. Clarifying the advantages and disadvantages of a course of action;
4. Stimulating interest in a topic;
5. Promoting understanding of the component parts of a topic;
6. Making use of a wide range of informed opinion.

C. Who are the personnel involved?

1. *The moderator* makes arrangements for the panel and guides the discussion. He should have enough knowledge about the topic to enable him to promote discussion and encourage learning. Two other desirable qualities are resourcefulness and flexibility.

2. *The panel members* are persons who have special knowledge of and interest in the topic to be discussed and the ability to verbalize their thoughts. They are selected to represent different points of view, backgrounds, and experience. They should be willing to converse in an informal way without preaching or debating.

The panel members are not necessarily experts. They may be persons whose experience qualifies them to speak with some authority. For example, the topic "Improving Cooperation in Our Community" could be discussed by a panel of recognized experts in community planning, community development, and social problems. It could also be profitably discussed by a panel made up of such lay persons as a minister, a school board member, a business man, a city councilman, a woman's club officer, and a representative of labor. In this case the panel is composed of persons who can speak with some authority as a result of their past experience and present responsibilities.

3. *The audience* is usually composed of persons interested in the topic to be discussed. Their intellectual levels and interests will vary considerably. Their presence at the meeting is an indication of some interest. It is essential to suit the discussion to the needs and interests of the audience, if learning is to occur. If controversial issues are involved, many audience members have firm opinions before they hear the discussion. Some know very little if anything about the topic while others are well informed. Some may not be aware of the existence of a problem, while others may be unable to identify the problem in terms of personal values.

D. What is the usual pattern of communication?

The diagram below shows (1) that the conversation flows among the panel members and the moderator, (2) that conversation is not necessarily routed through the moderator, and (3) that the audience members merely listen and observe.

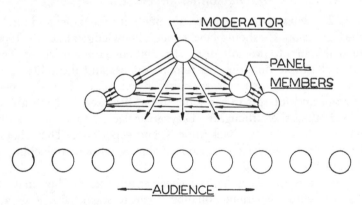

E. Advantages and limitations of the panel

1. *Advantages:*

a. Several competent resource persons can often stimulate more interest than one;

118

b. Different points of view can be expressed before the audience;

c. Panels usually have an atmosphere of informality;

d. A well-conducted panel can have a dramatic quality that stimulates interest and promotes learning.

2. *Limitations:*

a. The panel requires a moderator with skill in promoting and guiding discussion;

b. Several well-informed, effective panel members are not always available;

c. The audience members may not have enough interest, knowledge, and background to profit from the discussion;

d. An irresponsible panel member may use the occasion to promote personal advantage rather than to encourage learning;

e. Since the panel involves conversation, it sometimes does not lend itself to orderly, systematic presentation of information.

F. Check list for appraising the panel as a choice of technique

This list can be used in making the final decision as to whether or not the panel is an appropriate technique to use for a particular adult learning situation.

If the answers tend to be "no" or "undecided," consider using another technique.

	Yes	No	Unde-cided
1. Are we using the panel to:			
a. Identify and clarify problems or issues?	___	___	___
b. Bring several points of view before the audience?	___	___	___
c. Clarify the advantages and disadvantages of a course of action?	___	___	___
d. Stimulate interest in a topic?	___	___	___
e. Promote understanding of the component parts of a topic?	___	___	___
f. Make use of a wide range of informed opinion?	___	___	___

119

2. Can we:

a. Provide the proper physical set-up? ____ ____ ____

b. Insure audience comfort? ____ ____ ____

3. Do we have a topic about which there is a considerable range of informed opinion among the available panel members? ____ ____ ____

4. Do we have clear-cut goals to achieve? ____ ____ ____

5. Do we have a moderator who has the following qualifications:

a. Does he have enough knowledge about the topic and goals? ____ ____ ____

b. Can he instruct the panel members? ____ ____ ____

c. Can he promote effective discussion among the panel members? ____ ____ ____

d. Can he encourage active listening by the audience? ____ ____ ____

e. Does he understand the panel as a technique? ____ ____ ____

f. Can he remain neutral and yet show interest? ____ ____ ____

6. Do we have available panel members who:

a. Have the necessary knowledge? ____ ____ ____

b. Are interested in the topic(s)? ____ ____ ____

c. Can converse informally? ____ ____ ____

d. Can stay on the topic? ____ ____ ____

e. Keep in mind the needs and interests of the audience? ____ ____ ____

f. Can refrain from making speeches or talking too much? ____ ____ ____

7. Are we reasonably certain that audience participation will not be essential at this point? (If it is, the use of some other technique is preferable.) ____ ____ ____

8. Are there other techniques that might be more appropriate? ____ ____ ____

If yes, what are they and why? _____

_____

G. Responsibilities of the personnel involved in the panel

1. What does the moderator do?

a. *Prior to the meeting,* the moderator:

(1) Makes certain that he understands (a) the topic to be discussed, (b) the goals of the meeting or series of which the panel is a part, (c) the amount of time available for the panel, and (d) the technique he is employing;

(2) Studies the characteristics of the group that is anticipated. He considers the age, sex, background, and points of view of the audience members: What will they have in common and in what respects will their interest in and knowledge of the topic vary? What facts about the audience would help in instructing the panel members and guiding the discussion? How can the audience members be encouraged to listen carefully?

(3) Prepares some questions relating to the topic. These questions should be of interest to the audience and assist the moderator to start the discussion and keep it moving;

(4) Meets with the panel members prior to the meeting in order to:

(a) Get to know them, their backgrounds, and their points of view that relate to the topic,

(b) Explain to them their responsibilities, among which are: stick to the point, make short contributions rather than speeches, speak clearly, and converse in a lively spontaneous way,

(c) Help them understand the purposes and goals underlying the discussion they are to take part in and those of the meeting or series as a whole,

(d) Inform them about the characteristics of the expected audience;

(5) Makes preparations to insure that the proper physical set-up will be made;

(6) Explores the possibilities of encouraging the audience to do advance and follow-up study of helpful resource materials;

(7) Plans his introduction. The introduction should include:

(a) The topic and its importance,

(b) The purpose of the discussion,

(c) What the audience can expect to learn and the need for active listening on their part,

(d) The time limits of the discussion,

(e) The names and qualifications of the panel members;

(8) Decides whether or not it will be useful and practical to hold a brief "warm up" for the panel members immediately before the panel is conducted. One purpose of this meeting is to allow the moderator to get the feel of the discussion by conducting a brief conversation similar to the one that will be presented to the audience. Another purpose is to permit a review of such details as the names of the panel members, the goals of the panel, and the seating locations on the platform. If discussion of the topic is undertaken, the moderator should guard against the danger of the panel members getting so far into the discussion that much of the spontaneity will be lost in the presentation to the audience.

b. *During the panel discussion,* the moderator:

(1) Gives the introduction that he has prepared (see above);

(2) Tries to develop a friendly, informal atmosphere;

(3) Guides the discussion by offering comments and questions which keep the conversation lively and related to the topic;

(4) Provides opportunities for all panel members to converse;

(5) Guards against the domination of the conversation by one or two panel members;

(6) Remains neutral;

(7) Summarizes occasionally;

(8) Allows an appropriate amount of time for each question to be discussed;

(9) Tries to relate discussion to the knowledge and background of the audience by asking for elaboration, examples, and practical applications;

(10) Makes a final summary (if necessary);

(11) Encourages appropriate follow-up study and action by the audience.

2. *What do the panel members do?*

a. *Prior to the meeting,* the panel members:

(1) Familiarize themselves with this technique;

(2) Study the characteristics and needs of the group expected to be present;

(3) Try to understand the goals and the relationship of the panel in which they are to participate to the meeting or series as a whole;

(4) Prepare to participate flexibly and informally;

b. *During the panel discussion,* the panel members:

(1) Converse in a lively spontaneous way;

(2) Try to make their contributions meaningful to the audience;

(3) Keep their contributions brief and to the point;

(4) Refrain from dominating the discussion;

(5) Say "I don't know" when necessary.

3. *What does the audience do?*

a. *Prior to the meeting,* the audience should:

(1) Think about the topic and goals of the meeting;

(2) Do advance study (if appropriate);

(3) Try to understand the goals and the relationship of the panel to the meeting or series as a whole;

b. *During the panel discussion,* the audience should:

(1) Understand that this can be a learning experience if they participate intelligently as listeners;

(2) Try to relate the discussion to their own experience;

(3) Make a note of points about which they wish further explanation;

(4) Keep in mind the need for appropriate follow-up study and action.

H. *Physical arrangements and audience comfort*

1. *Physical set-up.*

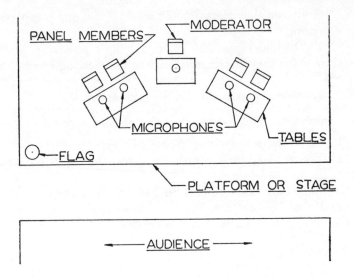

2. *Audience comfort.* Keep in mind the following points when making the arrangements:

a. Extremes in temperature can be distracting;

b. The audience should be comfortably seated;

c. The audience must be able to see and hear the moderator and panel members;

d. The audience and panel members should not face a glaring light;

e. Select a room or auditorium appropriate to the size of the group and the character of the meeting;

f. Provide a platform or stage if necessary;

g. Provide chairs and tables for the moderator and panel members;

h. Secure a public address system with individual microphones if necessary;

i. Provide *large* name cards to identify each panel member and the moderator.

I. How to evaluate after the panel has been conducted

The following check list will aid in appraising how effectively this technique has been conducted. It is for the use of (1) the persons who selected the panel as the appropriate technique and (2) those who took part in it.

It may be useful to have mimeographed or dittoed copies of the check list available for use after the panel has been presented.

If the replies tend to be "no" and "undecided," the panel probably has been used ineffectively; future errors can be avoided if the various replies are discussed briefly in a cooperative way.

	Yes	No	Unde-cided
1. Was the topic appropriate for discussion?	___	___	___
2. Was the physical set-up appropriate for this technique?	___	___	___
3. Did the moderator:			
a. Understand and properly instruct the panel members in the use of this technique?	___	___	___
b. Try to encourage the audience to listen carefully and relate the discussion to their experience?	___	___	___
c. Make clear the goals to be achieved?	___	___	___
d. Promote effective discussion among the panel members?	___	___	___
e. Adequately instruct the panel members?	___	___	___
4. Did the panel members:			
a. Have the necessary knowledge?	___	___	___
b. Discuss with the needs and interests of the audience in mind?	___	___	___
c. Stay on the topic?	___	___	___
d. Refrain from making speeches or talking too much?	___	___	___

5. Did the audience members:

a. Seem to be interested? _____ _____ _____

b. Listen attentively? _____ _____ _____

6. What was accomplished:

a. Were worthwhile points made in the discussion? _____ _____ _____

b. Did members of the audience show evidence of having acquired information, new viewpoints, or of having changed attitudes? _____ _____ _____

c. Did the audience make progress toward their goals? _____ _____ _____

d. Have problems or needs emerged which point toward further study or action? _____ _____ _____

e. Was there evidence of willingness to accept responsibility for further study or action? _____ _____ _____

7. Was the panel an appropriate technique for this learning situation? _____ _____ _____

What other techniques might have been effective and why? _____

_____

_____

J. How the panel might be used—an example

The planning committee for a workshop for high school history teachers wishes to encourage teachers to do more reading. They consider scheduling a speech by a college history teacher who might speak on the importance of reading. They reject this idea because no stimulating speaker is available at the time needed. They also feel that a more informal presentation is needed and that the topic lends itself to discussion. After inquiring, the committee identifies four high school history teachers who do a great deal of reading and seem to be well qualified to serve as members of a panel. A competent moderator is available, so the committee schedules a panel on the topic "Reading as an Adventure and a Professional Responsibility." The panel members are to converse about:

1. The kinds of reading they do;
2. How they find time to read;
3. Reading as a professional responsibility;
4. The rewards of reading.

This choice of technique may result in a stimulating presentation that motivates the audience member to increase the amount of reading that he does. The technique is appropriate because:

1. Several qualified panel members and a competent moderator are available;
2. The topic has discussable aspects;
3. It is desirable to stimulate interest with this presentation;
4. It is desirable to get the points of view of several persons;
5. Seeing and hearing four of their colleagues testify about the pleasures and value of reading may encourage reading on the part of the audience members.

IX. QUIET MEETING

A. *What is a quiet meeting?*

A quiet meeting is a 15 to 60 minute period of meditation and limited verbal expression by a group of five or more persons.

This technique is characterized by periods of silence and by occasional spontaneous verbal contributions by a member of the group. The periods of silence include meditation, concentration, and study about the topic which has been placed before them on a blackboard or easel. Freedom of expression is strongly encouraged.

When a participant wishes to share an idea, opinion, or reaction of any kind, he speaks. The participants do not necessarily react to or build upon each other's contributions as they do in group discussion. Also, they are under no obligation to talk.

The quiet meeting requires a group of persons who are not strangers to each other. It is usually not held at the outset of a series of educational activities. It is used at a point when the leaders or members feel that reflection and contemplation are desirable.

B. When should the quiet meeting be used?

This technique is used to accomplish one or more of the following purposes:

1. To promote personal reflection in a corporate setting;
2. To encourage people to clarify their thinking about a topic;
3. To provide an opportunity for people to relate ideas that have been presented in previous sessions;
4. To encourage the creative expression of ideas;
5. To permit the expression of personal feelings;
6. To enable the participants to gain new perspectives and refresh their minds when a meeting or series of meetings has ceased to be productive;
7. To re-establish a productive atmosphere when strong feelings have been aroused or a pointless argument has developed;
8. To provide a period of reflection in order to promote thoughtful discussion later;
9. To offer the participants opportunities to reflect before reaching conclusions or choosing a course of action;
10. To give a resource person (who listens and observes) the opportunity to study the needs and attitudes present in a group that he is assisting which could enable him to help more effectively in later activities of the group.*

C. Who are the personnel involved?

1. *The chairman* opens and closes the meeting. He does not lead discussion since the participants are not carrying on a discussion;
2. *The participants* are a rather closely knit group of 5 to 35 persons who are relatively comfortable in each other's presence (They should be persons who apparently are capable of bearing silence.);

D. What is the usual pattern of communication?

The participants do not converse, but rather they express their ideas and feelings. Therefore, almost all verbal contributions are

---

* If a resource person is present, he is *not* used to provide information during the quiet meeting.

made to the group as a whole. Except for his brief introduction and concluding remarks, the chairman's contributions are similar in character to those of the other participants.

The diagram below expresses:

1. That there are very few verbal contributions during the meeting;

2. That the speaking usually takes the form of isolated comments that are not directed to particular persons;

3. That many of the participants often remain silent;

4. That seating is not necessarily face-to-face.

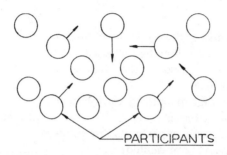

PARTICIPANTS

E. What are the advantages and limitations of the quiet meeting?

1. *Advantages:*

a. This technique can help us to learn to make creative use of silence and to place a premium on thinking;

b. A person can voluntarily express his needs in an uninhibited but thoughtful way;

c. A sense of fellowship can result from the silence and meditation;

d. A relatively deep level of thought can be reached.

2. *Limitations:*

a. Not all groups have members with enough self-discipline to get along without guidance by a leader;

b. Some people find it impossible to bear silence;

c. The required physical setting is not always available (a place that lends itself to reflection and meditation);

129

d. This technique requires that the participants have previously become acquainted.

F. A check list for appraising the quiet meeting as a choice of technique

This check list can be used in deciding whether or not the quiet meeting is an appropriate technique to use for a particular adult learning situation.

If the answers tend to be "no" or "undecided," consider using another technique.

	Yes	No	Unde-cided
1. Are we using the quiet meeting for one or more of the following purposes:			
a. To promote personal reflection in a corporate setting?	___	___	___
b. To encourage people to clarify their thinking about a topic?	___	___	___
c. To provide an opportunity for relating ideas previously presented?	___	___	___
d. To encourage the creative expression of ideas?	___	___	___
e. To permit the expression of personal feelings?	___	___	___
f. To enable a resource person to study the needs and attitudes of the participants?	___	___	___
g. To allow the participants to refresh their minds when a meeting or series of meetings has ceased to be productive?	___	___	___
h. To re-establish a productive atmosphere after a period of harmful tension?	___	___	___
i. To precede discussion by reflective thinking?	___	___	___
j. To encourage careful thinking before deciding on a course of action?	___	___	___
2. Do we have clear-cut goals to achieve?	___	___	___
3. Can we:			
a. Provide the proper physical set-up?	___	___	___

b. Insure audience comfort? ___ ___ ___

4. Can those who are to participate bear silence? ___ ___ ___

5. Will the participants be acquainted with each other? ___ ___ ___

6. Is the topic to be used one that does not require a resource person? ___ ___ ___

7. Is the topic of interest to all participants? ___ ___ ___

8. Is the size of the group expected to be from 5 to 35 persons? ___ ___ ___

9. Are there other techniques that might be more appropriate? ___ ___ ___

If yes, what are they? _____

_____

_____

G. Responsibilities of the personnel involved in the quiet meeting

1. *What does the chairman do?*

a. *Prior to the meeting,* the chairman:

(1) Makes certain that he understands the topic and its exact wording as selected by the planning committee or whoever arranged for the meeting;

(2) Selects and arranges the physical facilities for the meeting;

(3) Recommends to the participants (on some occasions) advance reading or thought about the topic;

(4) Tries to understand how this technique works.

b. *During the meeting,* the chairman:

(1) Explains the functioning of this technique to the participants, stressing the importance of periods of silence;

(2) Writes the topic on the blackboard or easel;

(3) States the amount of time available for the meeting (from 15 to 60 minutes);

(4) Performs the same role as that of any participant during the meeting itself. He need not speak at all;

(5) Closes the meeting at the specified time;

(6) Makes a few remarks, if need is indicated, at the end of the meeting, that give what he believes to have been the significance or implications of the meeting. This will depend on his judgment or previous instructions.

2. What do the participants do?

a. They may prepare for the meeting in any way that the chairman suggests or they consider appropriate;

b. They seek to understand this technique;

c. They speak only when they have a contribution that they feel will be of help to others or that they are especially anxious to express;

d. They use the long periods of silence as opportunities for reflection and meditation;

e. They do not feel obligated to build up each other's contribution;

f. They help to bring about an atmosphere of acceptance, fellowship, and mutual support.

H. Physical arrangements and group comfort

1. Physical set-up.

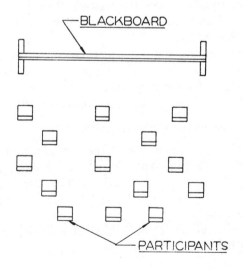

2. Group comfort.

a. The room should be one that is especially free from noise or distraction and appropriate to the size of the group;

b. The group can be seated around a table (or tables) arranged in a rectangle, seated in rows, or on chairs scattered throughout the room;

c. No person should face a glaring light;

d. Extremes in temperature are distracting;

e. Provide a blackboard, chalk, and eraser. An easel and paper with a large black crayon is equally useful.

I. How to evaluate after the quiet meeting has been held

The following check list should aid in appraising how effectively the quiet meeting has been conducted. It can be used by (1) the persons who selected this technique, and (2) those who take part in the quiet meeting.

It may be useful to have duplicated copies of the check list for use after the meeting has been held.

If the replies tend to be "no" and "undecided," the quiet meeting may well have been used ineffectively; future mistakes can be avoided if the reasons for the various answers are discussed briefly in a cooperative way.

	Yes	No	Unde-cided
1. Did we accomplish our goals?	___	___	___
2. Was the topic:			
a. Appropriate for the group?	___	___	___
b. Of interest to all participants?	___	___	___
c. Appropriate for consideration without the aid of a resource person?	___	___	___
3. Were the physical facilities and arrangements adequate?	___	___	___
4. Was the group able to use silence effectively?	___	___	___
5. Did people apparently feel free to express their ideas and feelings?	___	___	___

6. Did the chairman:
a. Give a brief, helpful introduction? ___ ___ ___
b. Carefully explain this technique? ___ ___ ___
c. Begin and close on time? ___ ___ ___
d. Refrain from acting as a discussion leader? ___ ___ ___

7. What was accomplished:
a. Were worthwhile points made? ___ ___ ___
b. Did the participants show evidence of having clarified ideas? ___ ___ ___
c. Was the silence refreshing? ___ ___ ___
d. Have problems or needs emerged which point toward further study or action? ___ ___ ___
e. Was there evidence of willingness to accept responsibility for further study or action? ___ ___ ___

8. Was the quiet meeting an appropriate technique for this situation? ___ ___ ___

What other techniques might have been effective and why? _____
_____
_____

J. How the quiet meeting might be used—examples

Here are examples of the use of this technique in two different settings:

1. *An industrial group* can hold a quiet meeting to encourage practical thinking and problem solving. The group can reflect together about a problem that has defied solution by other approaches. "Waste" is a serious continuing problem of many industries. A quiet meeting might be used by some employees and their superiors in an attempt to come up with some fresh answers to this problem. This unique technique might lead to the discovery of a new solution.

2. *A church group* can hold a quiet meeting to encourage meditation about or understanding of an insight, a religious teaching, or a moral precept. Here the emphasis would be on con-

templation in an atmosphere of fellowship and trust. In addition to speaking, the participant might express his feelings by reading aloud or singing.

(It should be noted also that the technique could just as well be used for reflection about a problem that confronts a church. A group of parents might hold a quiet meeting on a topic like "How Can We Make More Opportunities for Family Prayer?")

X. ROLE-PLAYING

A. What is role-playing?

Role-playing is a spontaneous portrayal (acting out) of a situation, condition, or circumstance by selected members of a learning group.

Role-playing emphasizes relationships among people. Role-playing is done by members of the learning group who try to portray typical attitudes, rather than by persons having special acting abilities. After a problem or situation has been illustrated by role-play, the learning group discusses and interprets the action through the use of another technique such as group discussion.

An outstanding feature of role-playing is the emotional impact that comes from observing or taking part in a dramatic presentation. The role-players, and those observing them, usually come closer to an actual experience of the feelings and reactions connected with the problem or situation than they would by reading or hearing an account of it. Role-playing is especially valuable as a technique for getting people in a frame of mind for self-examination.

1. A conversation between a school teacher, a principal, a parent, and a child with a disciplinary problem. The scene might show differing points of view about the problem and suggest different approaches to its solution.

2. Conflict arising from a grievance of a factory worker who feels that working conditions should be improved. The players might include the worker, his foreman, the shop superintendent, and the union steward, each of whom sees the problem from a different point of view.

3. Differences in aims and values among leaders in a local

church. The minister, a trustee, an elder, a deacon, the church superintendent, and the director of religious education might present points of view as to church needs which ought to have top priorities for programming and allotment of available funds.

B. When should role-playing be used?

Role-playing may be used:

1. To illustrate dramatically various aspects of an interpersonal problem in order that they can be discussed;

2. To promote the understanding of the viewpoints and feelings of other persons;

3. To discover how people might react under certain conditions;

4. To provide skills and training in such areas as problem-solving and diagnosis;

5. To encourage the audience member to gain insight into his own attitudes and behavior.

C. Who are the personnel involved?

1. *The leader* is the person who sets up the role-play. He should understand the uses and limitations of role-playing and be able to direct the entire learning experience;

2. *The role-players* are members of the group who volunteer or are selected to play roles. They do not need experience in acting (In fact it is better if they lack it, since the temptation to try for dramatic excellence should be avoided.);

3. *The audience* are those who observe the role-play in order to learn from it. They support the role-players in any necessary way and take part in the discussion that follows.

D. What is the usual pattern of communication?

Since role-playing is the acting out of a situation or incident with the audience observing, the players do not talk directly with the audience, but rather with each other, as in any dramatic presentation. Their main task is to try to put into words the attitudes of the persons they are playing and to see that their presentation can be seen and heard clearly at all times by all members of the audience. For these reasons the pattern of communication is not shown here with a diagram.

E. What are the advantages and limitations of role-playing?

1. *Advantages:*

a. A role-play usually stimulates the audience to listen and observe with interest;

b. Persons in the audience can often see themselves in the roles played and thereby gain in self-understanding;

c. By playing a role or observing, individuals come to understand how others think and feel under certain conditions;

d. This technique can result in a more vivid presentation than that which usually results from talking about a problem or situation;

e. This technique is especially useful for problem analysis involving feelings and attitudes.

2. *Limitations:*

a. This technique cannot be used to accomplish highly complex objectives; it must be restricted to simple, clear-cut problems and situations;

b. There is often the temptation to use role-playing as a gimmick rather than as a means to encourage and facilitate learning;

c. The technique requires alert, careful direction; it is not an easy one to use effectively;

d. The role-play must be supplemented by the effective use of other techniques;

e. The group may become so involved in the technique that they neglect subject matter or content;

f. Role-players may become so involved in their roles that they manifest emotions of deep personal significance;

g. The prospects of playing a role can cause fear and anxiety in the players;

h. Some groups of learners may reject this educational technique.

F. Check list for appraising role-playing as a choice of technique

This list can be used in making the final decision as to whether or not role-playing is an appropriate technique to use for a particular adult learning situation.

If the answers tend to be "no" or "undecided," consider using another technique.

	Yes	No	Unde-cided
1. Is the use of role-playing intended to accomplish one or more of the following:			
a. Illustrating a problem in order that it can be discussed intelligently?	___	___	___
b. Promoting understanding of the feelings and viewpoints of others?	___	___	___
c. Testing in advance how people may react under certain conditions?	___	___	___
d. Encouraging audience members better to understand their own attitudes and actions?	___	___	___
2. Is the problem or situation to be dealt with an appropriate one for the expected audience?	___	___	___
3. Is the problem or situation relatively clear-cut and simple?	___	___	___
4. Is the group so constituted that they are likely to resist using role-playing?	___	___	___
5. Will the physical conditions lend themselves to the use of this technique?	___	___	___
6. Are there clear-cut goals to achieve?	___	___	___
7. Is the leader qualified to set up and use role-play?	___	___	___
8. Can we provide for and lead an analysis and discussion of the role-play?	___	___	___
9. Are members of the group willing to play the various roles?	___	___	___

138

10. Are there other techniques that might be more appropriate choices? _____ _____ _____

If yes, what are they and why? _____

_____

_____

G. Roles and responsibilities of the personnel involved in role-playing

Listed here are the major steps in using role-playing as a learning technique: (1) defining the problem and visualizing the situation; (2) determining the roles to be played; (3) casting the characters; (4) briefing the players and the audience; (5) acting out the scene; (6) replaying the scene (if desirable); and (7) analyzing or interpreting the role-play (by means of another technique).

There are two ways that these steps can be taken: (1) the entire process is under the direction of a leader who plans and arranges for the role-play in advance of the meeting; or (2) the leader can assist the group in setting up a role-play as the need arises. It should be carefully noted that either approach demands that the acting out of the scene be spontaneous and unrehearsed. The difference in the two approaches lies in the extent to which the planning is done in advance of the meeting.

The explanation that follows is geared to the first approach in which the leader or a planning committee has set up the role-play prior to the meeting. However, a group setting up role-playing while a meeting is in progress should be guided through exactly the same procedural steps by the leader. In this case, all the following items would read something like this: "The leader assists the group to . . . define the problem, determine the roles, cast the characters," etc.

1. What does the leader do?

a. *Prior to the meeting,* the leader:

(1) Carefully studies the characteristics of the group that is anticipated. He considers age, sex, background, and attitudes of

139

those who will be present. He tries to envision their reaction to the role-play, including their familiarity with it.

If the group is expected to resist the use of this technique he may plan to minimize their resistance by introducing it in a manner that will not be threatening;

(2) Defines the problem and visualizes the situation to be portrayed. The problem and situation should be relatively simple since the role-play is not suitable for getting at either complex problems or a long series of related problems;

(3) Determines the roles to be played. The general characteristics of each role in the situation to be played should be carefully worked out and written down. The number of roles should be kept to a minimum (usually from two to five);

(4) Determines whether or not the scene shall be replayed and, if so, whether or not roles will be reversed or new "actors" will be used during the replay. A scene is replayed to contrast two ways of doing something or to show the effects of a change in the behavior of one or more of the players;

An example of this would be a role-play showing the "wrong way" for an employee to handle an angry customer, followed by the "right way." Sometimes in replaying a scene, roles are reversed. This means that a player who has just played one role now takes another. This is done in order to allow the player to experience the situation or problem from another point of view. The effects of the reversing of roles would probably be discussed by the audience following the role-play; the player who reversed roles would be asked about differences in his feelings and his reactions as he goes through the scene the second time. A scene should be replayed only for definite reasons;

(5) Casts the characters. He does not seek persons with acting ability since the technique does not call for excellent acting. It is permissible to encourage a person to take a role but no one should be unduly "pressured." Sometimes people take roles in which they feel at ease; sometimes they take roles that require them to use imagination and empathy. The leader must select his cast according to the situation to be portrayed and the players available;

(6) Briefs the players. Briefing may be oral or written. The leader decides how much each player is to be told about the role

140

he is to play. This will vary and depend on the goals and the situation to be portrayed. Sometimes a short written description of the role is given to each player.* The role-play is never rehearsed. The goals of the role-play, the situation, and the characterizations are explained to the players, but the action is spontaneous;

(7) Plans for the necessary physical arrangements:

(a) Will properties be needed?

(b) How should the role-play be staged so that all can see and hear?

(c) If another technique precedes the role-play, will a break be necessary to permit the players to make last-minute preparations?

(8) Prepares an introduction that will help the audience to understand:

(a) The goals of the role-play,

(b) The situation to be portrayed,

(c) Where the action is taking place,

(d) The roles (with fictitious names) and the person portraying each role,

(e) Any background information necessary for understanding the role-play,

(f) The responsibilities of the audience to:

—to avoid expecting too much of the players.

—to observe carefully.†

---

* For example: In a role-play dealing with a parent-teacher-child relationship, a description of the parent's role might be: *Mrs. Jones.* She is an intelligent, educated mother who is disturbed over her child's behavior. She is not the type who believes that her child can do no wrong. But she does feel that the teacher and the principal are mishandling her child's behavior problem.

In a role-play dealing with a problem between a minister and the officers of his church, a description of the minister's role might be: He is a young, energetic minister, fresh from seminary. He is anxious to build up and revitalize his church as quickly as possible. He is liable to interpret cautious advice by the church officers as a dragging of feet.

† Sometimes special assignments for observing are given. Part of the audience may be assigned to observe a particular player. Or a part of the audience may be asked to observe the action with one question in mind, while other observer "teams" observe with other questions in mind. For example, one group might be asked to keep this question in mind as they observe: "How would the situation be affected if Bill would listen to John's remarks and refrain from raising his voice?"

—to observe in terms of the goals and the kind of discussion or analysis scheduled to follow the role-play.

b. *Before, during and after the role-play is presented, the leader:*

(1) Checks physical arrangements;

(2) Gives final briefing to the players in a short "warm-up" period for getting in character;

(3) Presents his introduction to the audience;

(4) Calls for the action to begin;

(5) Cuts off the action at an appropriate time (as soon as the desired aspects of the problem or situation have been revealed);

(6) "Releases" the actors from their roles—usually by calling on each one who wishes to express how he felt in the role or make any comment he wishes (*Note:* it is especially important to forestall any player's getting too far into his role—that is, beginning to act as if he actually were the person being portrayed.);

(7) Calls for a replay of the scene if such a course has been agreed on in advance. The role-play may be discussed before the replay, or the two versions may be completed before the actors are released from their roles and the analysis is begun;

(8) Conducts an analysis or discussion of the action by use of another technique* (or turns the leadership of the meeting over to a person previously designated to do this).

2. *What does a role-player do?*

a. *Prior to the role-play,* the role-player:

(1) Accepts only roles that he feels are appropriate for him;

(2) Tries to understand the goals of the role-play;

(3) Tries to get the "feel" of the role he is to play.

b. *During the role-play,* the player:

(1) Assumes as nearly as he can the identity of the person he has agreed to play;

(2) Does not try to put on a great acting performance;

(3) Keeps in mind the goals of the role-play;

---

* For example, a panel might be used to discuss the role-play; a speech might be used for commentary on it; discussion groups might be set up; or a forum might be used to permit audience discussion with expert assistance.

(4) Tries to enjoy himself in the role without showing off or attempting to entertain the audience;

(5) Avoids getting too far into the role.

3. *What is expected of the audience?*

a. They should make appropriate preparation in the form of reading or thinking about the problem or situation;

b. They give moral support to the actors and do not evaluate or criticize the acting;

c. They should carefully observe the role-play in the light of the goals stated, and in the manner suggested, by the leader;

d. They should contribute to thoughtful analysis and discussion following the role-play.

H. *Physical arrangements and audience comfort*

1. *Physical set-up.*

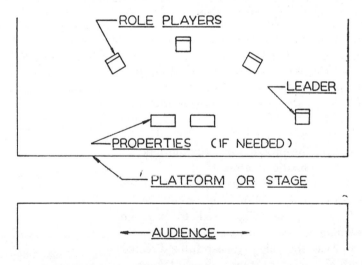

2. *Audience comfort.* Keep the following points in mind when making arrangements:

a. Extremes in temperature are distracting;

b. Select a room appropriate to the size of the group;

c. Provide platform or stage if necessary;

143

d. Audience members should not face a glaring light and must be able to see and hear at all times;

e. Provide a public address system if necessary (one microphone for each player); be sure to carefully test its operation in advance.

I. How to evaluate after the role-playing has been conducted

The following check list will aid in appraising how effectively the role-play has been conducted. It can be used by (1) the persons who selected this as the appropriate technique and (2) those who take part in and observe the role-play. It is useful to have mimeographed or dittoed copies of the check list for use when the role-play has been concluded.

If the replies tend to be "no" and "undecided," role-playing may well have been used ineffectively; future mistakes can be avoided if the reasons for the various answers are discussed briefly in a cooperative spirit.

	Yes	No	Unde-cided
1. Was the problem or situation portrayed of interest to the audience?	___	___	___
2. Were the physical arrangements adequate for the audience to see and hear the role-players?	___	___	___
3. Did the problem or situation lend itself to dramatic treatment?	___	___	___
4. Were the audience and the players given clear instructions and orientation?	___	___	___
5. Was role-playing used to promote learning rather than as a gimmick?	___	___	___
6. Was the role-play carefully directed with all necessary steps properly taken?	___	___	___
7. Did the role-players:			
a. Accept only appropriate roles?	___	___	___
b. Understand the goals of the role-play?	___	___	___
c. Assume the identity of the character assigned them?	___	___	___

d. Refrain from showing off or over-acting? ____ ____ ____

e. Avoid getting too far into their roles? ____ ____ ____

8. Was satisfactory analysis made of the role-play? ____ ____ ____

9. Did the audience members:

a. Make advance preparation? ____ ____ ____

b. Support the players and refrain from criticizing the acting? ____ ____ ____

c. Observe carefully? ____ ____ ____

d. Contribute thoughtful analysis or discussion? ____ ____ ____

10. What was accomplished:

a. Were worthwhile points made in the role-play? ____ ____ ____

b. Did members of the audience show evidence of having acquired information, new viewpoints, or of having changed attitudes? ____ ____ ____

c. Did the group make progress toward their goals? ____ ____ ____

d. Have problems or needs emerged which point toward further study or action? ____ ____ ____

e. Was there evidence of willingness to accept responsibility for further study or action? ____ ____ ____

11. Was the role-play an appropriate technique for this learning situation? ____ ____ ____

What other techniques might have been effective and why? _____

_____

_____

J. How role-playing might be used—an example

A small planning group of agricultural extension personnel and 4-H leaders have become concerned about a problem: Young adults in rural areas who do not go to college are facing a difficult adjustment. Modern technology is resulting in fewer and

145

fewer good jobs available in farming for persons who lack specialized training. The large efficient farm is replacing the small farm. As a result, in many rural communities there are numerous young adults (18-30 years of age) who face the future with uncertainty. They may not be trained for non-farm jobs. They may not know how to go about moving to another community to establish themselves.

Our planning committee intends to provide educational activities designed to meet this problem. They envision a series of evening meetings held in various private homes to assist these young adults to learn to face their problems with confidence.

It is clear that many of the young adults in question have problems that grow out of their living with parents and grandparents. In many cases the parents do not understand the technological changes that are taking place in farming. They may insist that their children remain to farm the property just as they and their forefathers did despite evidence that the farm will not be able to compete with the larger farms of the future.

The committee gradually realizes that at least one session will have to make use of a technique that dramatizes some of the interpersonal problems, relationships, and attitudes likely to be found in the homes of the young adults who will participate in the meetings. So the committee invites three of these young persons to assist in setting up role-plays that will bring out various problems and attitudes that emerge in the family situation. One role-play is to center on the problems arising when the young adult and his parents cannot agree with each other about the implications of the rapid changes in farming and rural life.

A situation is planned that will include the roles of a middle-aged farmer, his wife and his married son and his wife. They will carry on a family discussion that brings out differing attitudes toward a decision that the young couple must make. The young man has an opportunity to take a job in a factory far away. His father does not wish him to leave, despite the fact that the farm will not support two families. The young man's wife wishes him to take the job. His mother's opinion waivers between the two courses of action. The role-players will be given freedom to bring out whatever aspects of the problem they think are appropriate once the role-play is under way.

146

The use of this technique should:

1. Assist the learner to better understand similar problems that he faces;
2. Put the learner in a frame of mind that will encourage him to examine his own feelings and attitudes that may need changing;
3. Emphasize the interpersonal aspects of a problem of this kind;
4. Help the learner to grasp how persons like his parents think and feel about major adjustments.

Role-playing is the proper technique to use because:

1. The problem involves relationship among people and people's attitudes and feelings;
2. A dramatic illustration seems appropriate;
3. It should not be difficult to get people to take the various roles;
4. A person is available who knows how to conduct role-playing properly;
5. A competent leader is available to guide discussion following the role-play.

XI. Seminar

A. What is the seminar?

The seminar is a group of 5 to 30 persons engaged in specialized study and led by a recognized authority in the subject being studied.

The purpose of the seminar is to provide an opportunity for the participants to study a subject under the guidance of an authority. The study may be relatively advanced in character, with each seminar member doing individual study and reporting as suggested by the director. Usually the members prepare written or oral reports which they share with each other. A number of different educational procedures may be used in the seminar.

A typical session usually goes something like this:

147

Time	Technique	Purpose
15-30 minutes	Speech by Director	To present introductory information about the topic;
10-30 minutes	Reports by Members	To provide information about several phases of the topic, from the members' viewpoints, after consulting resource materials;
5 minutes	Question Period	To make certain that each report is understood;
20-30 minutes	Group Discussion	To synthesize and assimilate the information presented in the report(s) and permit conversation about the discussible aspects of the topic;
10-15 minutes	Speech by Director	To allow the director to correct erroneous ideas, suggest new ideas; and encourage further study and thought;
15 minutes	Planning and Assignments	To plan for future sessions.

B. When should the seminar be used?

The seminar may be used to:

1. Undertake careful study under the guidance of a well-qualified authority;

2. Reach a conclusion based on thorough investigation;

3. Present information systematically;

4. Discuss or lay out necessary research for the solution of a problem;

5. Identify and explore problems.

148

C. Who are the personnel involved?

1. *The director* of the seminar is chosen for his extensive knowledge in the area to be studied and his ability to assist others to learn. He is in charge of the seminar at all times. He alternately takes the roles of coordinator, teacher, resource person, and discussion leader. He should understand which role is appropriate at a particular time and how to carry it out. He should know how to direct individual and group study, how to encourage interest, and how to help others to accept their share of responsibility for study and discussion. He should have the desire to learn as well as teach and look on the seminar as a personal learning opportunity;

2. *The seminar members* are usually persons with similar knowledge and background. They should be interested in the topic and willing to undertake systematic, thoughtful study and discussion.

D. What is the usual pattern of communication?

We have said that one feature of the seminar is the presentation of information by the director of the seminar and the members. Obviously, when a speech is underway or when someone is reading a paper, the verbal communication is merely one way as in the diagram for speech (see p. 158).

At other times, however, the verbal communication is characterized by free interchange among the members and between the members and the director as the following diagram shows.

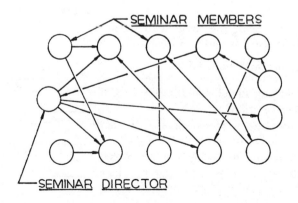

SEMINAR MEMBERS

SEMINAR DIRECTOR

E. *Advantages and limitations of the seminar*

1. *Advantages:*

a. A recognized expert or authority is available to assist the learners;

b. Careful, systematic inquiry and discussion can take place;

c. Active participation is stimulated, not only in the discussion period, but through the preparation and presentation of reports.

2. *Limitations:*

a. It is often difficult to obtain a person who has the necessary qualifications to direct the seminar;

b. Members may refuse to spend the time required for preparing adequate reports;

c. Appropriate resource materials may not be available;

d. Members may be reluctant to participate verbally when given the chance. The presence of an expert may inhibit them.

F. *Check list for appraising the seminar as a choice of technique*

This list can be used as a help in deciding whether or not the seminar is an appropriate technique to use for a particular adult learning situation.

If the answers tend to be "no" or "undecided," consider using another extended technique.

	Yes	No	Unde-cided
1. Are we using the seminar to accomplish one or more of the following:			
a. Encouraging thoughtful study under expert direction?	___	___	___
b. Reaching conclusions based on thorough investigation?	___	___	___
c. Presenting information systematically?	___	___	___
d. Discussing or laying out research?	___	___	___
e. Identifying and exploring problems?	___	___	___

2. Is our topic an appropriate one for the group? _____ _____ _____

3. Do we have clear-cut goals to achieve? _____ _____ _____

4. Are the necessary resource materials available? _____ _____ _____

5. Can we provide the necessary physical set-up and insure the comfort of those participating? _____ _____ _____

6. Do we have a director available who:

a. Knows thoroughly the area to be studied and its resource materials? _____ _____ _____

b. Can plan a seminar? _____ _____ _____

c. Knows how to direct individual and group study? _____ _____ _____

d. Shows interest and enthusiasm for his subject? _____ _____ _____

e. Knows how to use appropriately such techniques as the speech, question period, and group discussion? _____ _____ _____

f. Can encourage people to accept responsibility? _____ _____ _____

g. Can present information effectively? _____ _____ _____

7. Are the potential seminar members:

a. Similar in background and knowledge about the topic to be studied? _____ _____ _____

b. Willing to study systematically? _____ _____ _____

c. Willing to participate actively? _____ _____ _____

8. Are there other techniques that might be more appropriate choices? _____ _____ _____

If yes, what are they and why? _____

_____

_____

G. Responsibilities of the personnel involved in the seminar

1. What does the director do?

a. *Prior to the seminar,* the director:

(1) Plans the course of study with the needs and interests of the members in mind;

(2) Makes arrangements for necessary materials and facilities;

(3) Suggests advance preparation to the members;

(4) Assigns readings and suggests provocative discussion questions;

(5) Seeks to clarify the purpose and goals of the seminar;

(6) Thinks about the characteristics of the group he will be working with in order to identify needs and interests that might help him to encourage study and discussion;

(7) Considers techniques, devices, and educational aids to be used for presenting information and promoting discussion;

(8) Prepares his introductory speech.

b. *During the seminar,* the director:

(1) Presents the introductory speech he has prepared;

(2) Tries to communicate enthusiasm and interest as well as ideas;

(3) Respects the adult's individual dignity and rights;

(4) Leads or directs someone else in the leading of the question period, the group discussion, and other techniques which may be used;

(5) Asks participants to present their reports;

(6) Avoids acting exclusively as a teacher—the ideal is a teaching-learning relationship in which all are learning together;

(7) Offers resource information on request or at appropriate times;

(8) Avoids preaching, pontificating, and showing off his broad knowledge;

(9) Encourages different points of view;

(10) Assists the members to select individual topics for future study;

152

(11) Assists each member to prepare his report;

(12) Comments on each report;

(13) Leads (or asks for a qualified volunteer to lead) a discussion following each report;

(14) Encourages continued study after the close of the seminar;

(15) Supervises the arrangement and reproduction of the findings in a report (if this is to be done).

2. What do the seminar members do?

a. *Prior to the seminar,* the members:

(1) Try to understand the goals of the seminar;

(2) Do whatever study and thinking are recommended by the seminar director;

(3) Prepare clear and logical report(s) to the seminar, if requested;

(4) Seek to understand the workings of this technique (the seminar);

(5) Prepare themselves for learning.

b. *During the seminar,* the members:

(1) Accept responsibility for individual study and for the success of the seminar;

(2) Select specific topics for individual study;

(3) Present oral or written reports clearly and logically;

(4) Help the director to avoid becoming an excessively authoritarian teacher;

(5) Listen actively and participate in one of the many ways open to them:

(a) Request clarification,

(b) Offer ideas and opinions,

(c) Prepare reports,

(d) Build on the contributions of others,

(e) Offer suggestions for modifying or improving the seminar,

(f) Seek solutions to problems and assist others in their search.

H. Physical arrangements and group comfort

1. *Physical set-up.*

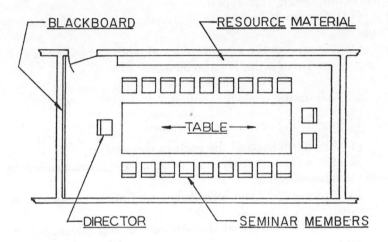

2. *Group comfort.*

a. Extremes in temperature are distracting;

b. Comfortable seats can be helpful;

c. No one should face a glaring light;

d. Room should be of appropriate size, permitting materials and worktable to be available continuously;

e. Provide blackboards, projector, and screen (if necessary);

f. Room should be free of distracting noises;

g. Provide a crayon and a 5 x 8 card on which each person can print his name.

I. How to evaluate after the seminar has been conducted

The following check list will aid in appraising how effectively this technique has been conducted. It is for the use of (1) the persons who selected the seminar as the appropriate technique and (2) those who take part in it.

It may be useful to have mimeographed or dittoed copies of the check list available for use after the seminar.

154

If the replies tend to be "no" and "undecided," the seminar probably has been used ineffectively; future errors can be avoided if the various replies are discussed briefly in a cooperative way.

	Yes	No	Unde-cided
1. Was the topic of the seminar an appropriate one for the group to study?			
2. Were the physical arrangements conducive to the comfort of the group and to effective learning?			
3. Were the necessary resource materials available?			
4. Were appropriate educational aids selected?			
5. Were educational aids used effectively?			
6. Were the seminar members:			
a. Sufficiently similar in background and knowledge?			
b. Informed about the topic prior to the beginning of the seminar?			
c. Willing to do sustained, systematic study?			
d. Effective participants in discussion?			
e. Willing to make reports?			
7. Did the director of the seminar:			
a. Assist the group to understand the use of this technique?			
b. Have clear-cut goals which he shared with the group?			
c. Do adequate planning?			
d. Know thoroughly the area under study?			
e. Present his information effectively?			
f. Know how to assist others to learn?			
g. Effectively use various educational techniques?			

h. Experience difficulty in alternately serving as teacher, resource person, and discussion leader? ____ ____ ____

i. Refrain from showing off his knowledge? ____ ____ ____

8. What was accomplished:

a. Did the seminar members show evidence of having acquired information, new viewpoints, or changed attitudes? ____ ____ ____

b. Did the seminar members make progress toward their goals? ____ ____ ____

c. Have problems or needs emerged which point toward further study or action? ____ ____ ____
____ ____ ____

d. Was there evidence of willingness to accept responsibility for further study or action? ____ ____ ____

9. Was the seminar an appropriate technique for this situation? ____ ____ ____

10. What other techniques might have been effective and why? _____
_____
_____

J. How the seminar might be used—an example

A county council of social agencies has 30 members. The members are lay leaders and professional persons such as executive secretaries for the Girl Scouts, Y.M.C.A., Red Cross, Council of Churches, and Boys' Club. One aspect of the council's work is to provide opportunities for the self-education of its members. A considerable portion of the regular monthly meeting is usually given over to educational activities.

They usually hold general meetings. However, someone points out that the general meetings can only scratch the surface of this broad and vital topic ("Trends in Our Society That Have Implications for Social Agencies"). The group decides that this is a topic which requires guided study over an extended period of time. They arrange for a series of seminars, each under the direction of a qualified expert. This will enable all of the council members who are really concerned to explore the topic in depth.

XII. Speech

A. *What is the speech?*

A speech is a carefully prepared oral presentation of a subject by a qualified person. It is frequently referred to as a lecture.

This technique appears to be easy to use. However, for productive learning, the program using the speech requires careful planning.

B. *When should the speech be used?*

The speech may be the technique to use when your topics and goals point toward doing one or more of the following:

1. Presenting information in an organized way;
2. Identifying or clarifying problems or issues;
3. Presenting analysis of a controversial issue;
4. Stimulating or inspiring the audience;
5. Encouraging further study or inquiry.

C. *Who are the personnel involved?*

1. *The chairman* arranges for the speech and presides over it. He should be able to plan this assignment. He should possess a reasonably good speaking voice. A sense of humor is helpful. The person who serves as chairman for the entire meeting can also act as chairman for the speech, if he has the necessary qualifications;

2. *The speaker* should be well informed about the topic he is treating and able to relate his presentation to the needs and interests of the audience. He must be capable of delivering a well-organized speech within the time limit using language that the audience understands;

3. *The audience* is usually composed of persons interested in the topic to be presented. The extent of their knowledge and the degree of their interest will vary from person to person. Their presence at the meeting is an indication of some interest. If controversial issues are involved, many of the persons in the

audience will have made up their minds one way or another before they come to the meeting. Some will know very little if anything about the topic and others will be better informed. The audience may contain persons who do not recognize the existence of a problem or are unable to identify the problem in terms of personal opinions or values. The audience may also include persons who know something about the issues to be presented but who have not come to any definite conclusions.

D. What is the usual pattern of communication?

Since the speaker and the chairman do the talking, this technique is characterized by verbal communication that flows in one direction—from the platform to the audience. The following diagram shows this pattern.

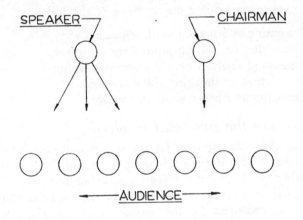

E. Advantages and limitations of the speech

1. *Advantages:*

a. Facts and opinions can be presented in an orderly systematic way;

b. Educational aids can readily be used by a speaker to accompany the presentation;

c. A skillful speaker can stimulate and motivate the participants to further study and inquiry;

158

d. Large numbers of persons can be accommodated with this technique;

e. Information can be made available to persons who will not, or cannot, use printed materials.

2. *Limitations:*

a. Only one person's ideas, background, and point of view are presented;

b. The audience has no opportunity for verbal participation;

c. The effects of the speech upon the audience cannot be easily determined;

d. A careless or irresponsible speaker may distort facts;

e. The speaker may use words that people cannot understand;

f. Some speakers are more interested in making a speech than in helping people to learn.

F. Check list for appraising the speech as a choice of technique

This list can be used in making the final decision as to whether or not the speech is an appropriate technique to use for a particular adult learning situation.

If the answers tend to be "no" or "undecided," you should consider using another technique.

	Yes	No	Unde-cided
1. Are we using the speech in order to accomplish one or more of the following:			
a. Identifying or clarifying problems or issues?	___	___	___
b. Analyzing a controversial issue?	___	___	___
c. Presenting information in an organized way?	___	___	___
d. Stimulating or inspiring the audience?	___	___	___
e. Encouraging further study or inquiry?	___	___	___
2. Have clear-cut goals been achieved?	___	___	___

3. Are we reasonably certain that verbal participation by the audience is not essential at this point in the program? ____ ____ ____

4. Can we provide the necessary physical set-up and insure audience comfort? ____ ____ ____

5. Do we have a speaker with these qualifications:

a. Knowledge of the topic? ____ ____ ____

b. Ability to use words and examples that the audience understands? ____ ____ ____

c. Ability to make an organized presentation? ____ ____ ____

d. Ability to stay within the time limit? ____ ____ ____

e. Willingness to try to speak to the needs and interests of the audience? ____ ____ ____

6. Is a chairman available who can:

a. Plan with the speaker and carefully instruct him concerning his responsibilities? ____ ____ ____

b. Introduce the speech effectively? ____ ____ ____

c. See that the speaker stays within the allotted time limit? ____ ____ ____

7. Are there other techniques that might be more appropriate choices? ____ ____ ____

If yes, what are they and why? _____

_____

_____

G. Responsibilities of the personnel involved in the speech

1. *What does the chairman do?*

a. *Prior to the meeting,* the chairman:

(1) Carefully studies the characteristics of the anticipated audience. He considers their age, sex, background, and possible points of view toward the topic to be presented. What will they have in common and in what respects will their knowledge and

interests vary? What are the implications for instructing the speaker and introducing the speech?

(2) Meets with the speaker* in order to:

(a) Get to know enough about him to make an effective introduction,

(b) Explain the topics and goals of the speech and its intended length,

(c) Find out the speaker's plans regarding the use of educational aids,

(d) Find out whether or not the speaker would like to use a lectern and a public address system;

(3) Prepares an introduction that will make clear:

(a) The topic—why it is important and how it relates to the lives of audience members,

(b) The purposes of the speech—what the listener hopes to gain by active listening,

(c) The reasons for using this technique,

(d) The name, title, background, and qualifications of the speaker,

(e) The relationships between the speech and other parts of the program (or series) that may have preceded it or that may follow it,

(f) The intended length of the speech.

b. *During the meeting*, the chairman:

(1) Gives his introduction with interest and cordiality;

(2) Makes appropriate remarks at the close of the speech:

(a) Relating the speech to the over-all goals and topics for the meeting or series,

(b) Encouraging the audience to further study,

(c) Thanking the speaker;

(3) Closes the meeting or turns over its direction to the appropriate person.

---

* A less satisfactory way of instructing the speaker is by letter. When it is necessary to carry on the instruction by mail, information should be very clearly stated.

2. *What does the speaker do?*

a. *Prior to the meeting,* the speaker:

(1) Plans to meet the needs and interests of the audience and keeps in mind the goals the speech is to achieve;

(2) Plans to stay within the time allowed;

(3) Plans for the use of educational aids if desirable;

(4) Plans appropriate examples and illustrations;

(5) Meets any agreed-upon deadline for submitting written draft of his speech;

(6) Plans to use ideas, vocabulary, and examples appropriate to the background and experience of the audience.

b. *During the meeting,* the speaker:

(1) Makes a logical, orderly presentation;

(2) Uses appropriate vocabulary and illustrative examples;

(3) Observes audience reaction to his presentation in the hopes of making his speech as meaningful as possible;

(4) Stays within alloted time limit.

3. *What is expected of the audience?*

a. *Prior to the meeting,* the audience members:

(1) Should prepare by reading appropriate materials and thinking about the topic to be covered in the speech;

(2) Should try to understand the goals the speech is to achieve and the goals of the meeting or series.

b. *During and after the speech,* the audience members:

(1) Should listen actively;

(2) Try to relate the speech to their own experience;

(3) Keep in mind the goals of the speech;

(4) Undertake appropriate follow-up study and action.

H. Physical arrangements and audience comfort

1. Physical set-up.

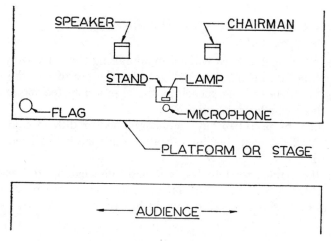

2. *Audience comfort.* Keep the following points in mind when making arrangements:

a. Provide platform or stage if needed;

b. Adequate seating arrangements for the speaker and the chairman should be provided on the stage or platform;

c. Provide a speaker's stand (if speaker wishes to use one) and sufficient light for him to see his notes;

d. Secure a public address system if necessary;

e. Extremes in temperature are distracting;

f. Audience should be comfortably seated;

g. Audience must not face glaring light;

h. Audience must be able to see and hear the speaker; the speaker should be able to see the entire audience;

i. Select a room or auditorium appropriate to the size of the group and the character of the meeting;

j. If such educational aids as maps, charts, graphs, films, slides, and blackboard are to be used, consider carefully their suitability, their location, and visibility to the entire audience:

(1) Educational aids can detract from the speech if allowed to remain in front of the audience after being used;

(2) If a projector is used, an electrical outlet must be available. The outlet should be tested prior to the meeting to see if it functions when the lights are turned off.

I. How to evaluate after the speech has been presented

The following check list will aid in appraising how effectively this technique has been conducted. It is for the use of (1) the persons who selected the speech as the appropriate technique and (2) those who hear the speech.

It may be useful to have mimeographed or dittoed copies of the check list available for use after the speech has been presented.

If the replies tend to be "no" and "undecided," the speech probably has been used ineffectively; future errors can be avoided if the various replies are discussed briefly in a cooperative way.

	Yes	No	Unde-cided
1. Was the speaker's presentation:			
a. Delivered in an organized way?	___	___	___
b. Understood by the audience?	___	___	___
c. Related to the interests and needs of the audience?	___	___	___
d. Suited to the intended goals?	___	___	___
e. Appropriate in length?	___	___	___
2. Were appropriate visual aids employed?	___	___	___
3. Were visual aids used effectively?	___	___	___
4. Was the physical set-up right for effective use of this technique?	___	___	___
5. Was audience comfort sufficiently provided for?	___	___	___
6. Did the chairman:			
a. Successfully instruct the speaker?	___	___	___
b. Effectively introduce the topic and the speaker?	___	___	___
c. Include the necessary information in his introduction?	___	___	___

d. Encourage the audience to listen actively? ___ ___ ___

e. See that the speech ended on time? ___ ___ ___

7. Did the audience appear to:

a. Have made advance preparation and study? ___ ___ ___

b. Listen with interest? ___ ___ ___

8. Were there times during the speech when audience participation seemed desirable? ___ ___ ___

9. What was accomplished: ___ ___ ___

a. Were worthwhile points made in the speech? ___ ___ ___

b. Did members of the audience show evidence of having acquired information, new viewpoints, or of having changed attitudes? ___ ___ ___

c. Did the group make progress toward their goals? ___ ___ ___

d. Have problems or needs emerged which point toward further study or action? ___ ___ ___

e. Was there evidence of willingness to accept responsibility for further action? ___ ___ ___

10. Was the speech an appropriate technique for this situation? ___ ___ ___

What other techniques might have been effective and why? _____

_____

_____

J. How the speech might be used—an example

A national organization, like the Red Cross, operates by means of an administrative plan that is based on regions or districts. It is customary for the local representatives in each district to come together periodically for in-service training meetings. At one district meeting the group wishes to learn about a new practice adopted by the organization. The only available person with knowledge about the new practice is the district vice-president. He is a capable and stimulating speaker and will have available some educational aids useful in explaining the new practice.

Since some of the information is technical, an interview as a technique does not seem appropriate. Since the audience members will have little or no knowledge about the topic, a colloquy is not a logical choice. The speech is selected as the appropriate technique because:

1. Only one qualified person is available to present the information;
2. Appropriate educational aids are available;
3. The learning situation calls for a clear explanation.

XIII. Symposium (Ancient Concept)

A. What is the symposium (ancient concept)?

A symposium is a group of 5 to 20 persons who meet in a home or private dining room to enjoy good food, entertainment, fellowship, and with the desire to discuss informally a topic of mutual interest.

After the group has begun eating, the previously selected topic is introduced by the symposiarch (the moderator). The group members are then free to talk informally about the topic if they wish. When everyone has finished eating and the table has been cleared, the group carries on a more systematic but informal discussion of the topic under the guidance of the symposiarch.

As a rule, this technique is used for leisurely exploration of a topic rather than problem-solving or discussing highly controversial issues.

B. When should the symposium (ancient concept) be used?

This educational technique can be used when it is desirable to accomplish one or more of the following:

1. To provide a complete program (i.e., social activity, food, entertainment, and discussion);

2. To examine or explore the component parts of a topic or topics;

3. To offer opportunities for self-expression;

4. To encourage persons with similar interests to exchange ideas in an informal and friendly atmosphere;

5. To provide an opportunity for husband and wife to associate with friends;

6. To encourage study and discussion of interest areas usually not considered in our work-a-day lives.

C. Who are the personnel involved?

1. *The symposiarch* is the presiding member of the meeting. He should be selected for his ability to plan and carry out the details of the meeting. He should be able to encourage people to enjoy themselves but at the same time be able to guide the discussion. A sense of humor is very helpful.

2. *The participants* are the 5 to 20 persons invited to take part; they are congenial and interested in exchanging ideas about the topic(s) to be considered.

D. What is the usual pattern of communication?

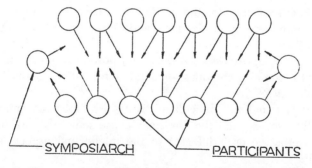

SYMPOSIARCH   PARTICIPANTS

This diagram reveals (through the arrows) how the conversation flows among those participating. The diagram shows that there can be verbal participation by all. It shows that, while contributions should be offered to the group as a whole, a brief interchange between two participants is permissible.

As a rule, the symposiarch recognizes persons before they speak, but spontaneous contributions are also in order. The extent to which he exercises control of the discussion will vary with (1) the difficulty of the topic, (2) the size of the group, and (3) the ability of the participants to accept responsibility for productive discussion.

E. Advantages and limitations of the symposium

1. *Advantages:*

a. Eating together in an informal setting tends to eliminate real or imaginary social and intellectual barriers and to foster free exchange of ideas;

b. Food, music, and mutual interests can result in a pleasant learning situation that is likely to be free from excessive conflict and controversy;

c. All persons present have opportunities for verbal participation;

d. Timid or shy persons are inclined to enter into discussion with this technique;

e. The opportunity is available for each person to develop an idea rather fully.

2. *Limitations:*

a. It is necessary for the participants to have relatively much in common, as regards interests and knowledge of the topic(s) to be discussed;

b. As a rule, discussion is not as purposeful or direct in intent as with some techniques—general information tends to be brought out;

c. It is sometimes difficult to distinguish fact from opinion;

d. The setting and the food may cause some of those present to be lethargic or indifferent to the intellectual aspects of the meeting;

e. Only a relatively small number of persons can be involved.

F. Check list for appraising the symposium as a choice of technique

This list can be used in making the final decision as to whether or not the symposium is an appropriate technique to use for a particular adult learning situation.

If the answers tend to be "no" or "undecided," consider using another technique.

	Yes	No	Unde-cided
1. Is this technique being used to accomplish one or more of the following:			
a. To provide a complete, well-rounded program?	___	___	___
b. To examine or explore the component parts of a topic?	___	___	___
c. To offer each person opportunities for self-expression?	___	___	___
d. To avoid excessive conflict and controversy?	___	___	___
2. Do we have clear-cut goals to achieve?	___	___	___
3. Do we have a topic that:			
a. Is appropriately worded for discussion?	___	___	___
b. Is of interest to all participants?	___	___	___
c. Is within the knowledge and range of experience of all participants?	___	___	___
d. Lends itself to relaxed, leisurely exploration?	___	___	___
4. Can we provide adequate physical arrangements including music and good food and surroundings free from noise and other distractions?	___	___	___
5. Do we have available a symposiarch to do the following:			
a. See that the necessary arrangements are made?	___	___	___
b. Prepare questions to stimulate discussion?	___	___	___
c. Establish a cordial atmosphere free from tension?	___	___	___
d. Guide the discussion smoothly and with firmness?	___	___	___

169

6. Are there other techniques that might
be more appropriate? _____ _____ _____

If yes, what are they and why? _____

_____

_____

G. *Responsibilities of the personnel involved in the symposium*

1. *What does the symposiarch do?*

a. *Prior to the meeting*, the symposiarch:

(1) Plans the meeting and sees that the necessary arrange-ments are made for the meal, the music, the seating of the par-ticipants, and other details;

(2) Selects, with the approval of the group or planning com-mittee, a topic to be discussed. (If a planning committee has previously selected the topic, the symposiarch makes certain that he understands it thoroughly.) The topic should be one that the group can discuss comfortably; it should be worded so as to en-courage cooperative discussion and be related to the background and experience of the participants;

(3) Makes certain that he understands the mechanics of the symposium and the intended length of the one he is to lead (The recommended length is one and one half to two hours);

(4) Prepares some questions that will stimulate discussion. The questions should be clearly related to the topic;

(5) Carefully studies the characteristics of the group that is anticipated. He reflects about the age, sex, background, and points of view of the participants: what will they have in com-mon? in what respects will their interest and knowledge of the topic vary? What implications can be drawn for the conduct of the symposium?

(6) Suggests appropriate advanced reading to the participants, if it seems advisable to do so;

(7) Plans to encourage follow-up study and action. He may obtain materials to distribute for further study;

(8) Prepares an introduction that will:

(a) Clarify the topic and purpose of the discussion,

(b) Encourage participation by all,

(c) Provide necessary background information,

(d) Relate the topic to the experience of the participants,

(e) Establish a cordial atmosphere.

b. *During the meeting,* the symposiarch:

(1) Attends to such details as seating and introductions;

(2) Presents his introduction to the topic for discussion (see above);

(3) Presides in an informal and friendly manner, acting as a guide or helper rather than director;

(4) Recognizes one person at a time (When the size of the group is relatively large—about 12 persons—and demand for opportunity to speak is relatively strong, the symposiarch exercises rather firm control of the discussion.);

(5) Encourages and develops group participation;

(6) Tries to prohibit talkative persons from monopolizing the conversation, and avoids talking too much himself;

(7) Enters the discussion as a participant as well as leader. Since the symposiarch is considered a member of the group, he can offer ideas and opinions if he so desires.

2. *What do the participants do?*

a. *Prior to the meeting,* the participants:

(1) Should read appropriate materials on the topic(s) to be discussed if such readings have been suggested;

(2) Should accept responsibility for the success of the meeting and offer to help the symposiarch with arrangements.

b. *During the meeting,* the participants:

(1) Participate thoughtfully and voluntarily in the discussion;

(2) Keep the discussion related to the topic(s) under consideration;

(3) Bring out various aspects of the topic(s);

(4) Are informal and friendly in their relationships;

(5) Avoid monopolizing the conversation or showing off;

(6) Respect the opinions and points of view of all participants;

(7) Undertake follow-up study and action, if appropriate.

H. Physical arrangements and audience comfort

1. Physical set-up.

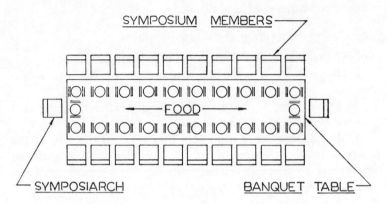

2. Audience comfort. Keep the following in mind when making arrangements:

a. Extremes in temperature should be avoided;

b. Group should be comfortably seated around the dinner table with no one facing a glaring light;

c. The menu should take into account the tastes and dietary restrictions of all persons participating;

d. Secure the necessary equipment and/or the personnel for the musical portion of the program (A record player can be used; sometimes one or more musicians play.);

e. Provision should be made for the removal, following the meal, of all items not to be used in the discussion period;

f. Provide a name card for each person, if the participants are not already acquainted with each other.

I. How to evaluate after the symposium has been conducted

The following check list will aid in appraising how effectively this technique has been conducted. It is for the use of (1) the persons who selected the symposium and (2) those who take part in it.

You may wish to have mimeographed or dittoed copies of the check list available for use after the symposium.

If the replies tend to be "no" and "undecided," the symposium probably has been used ineffectively; future errors can be avoided if the various replies are discussed briefly in a cooperative way.

	Yes	No	Unde-cided
1. Was the physical set-up adequate and free from distractions?	___	___	___
2. Was adequate comfort provided for?	___	___	___
3. Were the food and music satisfactory?	___	___	___
4. Did the topic for discussion turn out to be:			
a. Appropriately worded?	___	___	___
b. Of interest to all participants?	___	___	___
c. Within the knowledge of all participants?	___	___	___
d. Conducive to friendly, leisurely exploration?	___	___	___
5. Did the symposiarch:			
a. See that physical arrangements were made?	___	___	___
b. Prepare questions to stimulate discussion?	___	___	___
c. Promote advance study and follow-up study or action?	___	___	___
d. Establish a cordial, relaxed atmosphere?	___	___	___
e. Guide the discussion smoothly and with firmness?	___	___	___
6. Did the participants:			
a. Assist the symposiarch with the arrangements?	___	___	___
b. Show evidence of advance preparation?	___	___	___
c. Discuss the topic effectively?	___	___	___
d. Agree to undertake follow-up study or action?	___	___	___

7. What was accomplished:

a. Were worthwhile points made in the discussion? ___ ___ ___

b. Did members of the audience show evidence of having acquired information, new viewpoints, or of having changed attitudes? ___ ___ ___

c. Did the group make progress toward their goals? ___ ___ ___

d. Have problems or needs emerged which point toward further study or action? ___ ___ ___

e. Was there evidence of willingness to accept responsibility for further study or action? ___ ___ ___

8. Was the colloquy an appropriate technique for this situation? ___ ___ ___

What other techniques might have been effective and why? _____

_____

_____

J. How the symposium might be used—an example

A study group of 20 persons has been meeting twice a month in a public library to discuss current political issues. About halfway through the winter, the group realizes that interest is falling off. The group appraises its progress by means of a discussion of the topic "How Can We Revitalize Our Meetings?" Several ways of injecting interest are identified through this discussion, among them the suggestion that an occasional meeting be held in the home of one of the group members. It is felt that meetings in a home might lend an air of informality and encourage more active participation by some of the persons who have been hesitant to join in the discussion.

So the next meeting is planned as an ancient symposium. The scheduled topic is one that will lend itself to discussion that is spontaneous and more like general conversation than what has prevailed so far in the group's meetings. The symposium is held at the home of a husband and wife (new to the community) that

174

joined the group after it was in progress and have always remained somewhat as outsiders. Responsibility for the menu and music is accepted by a young man who also has been reluctant to participate verbally in the discussions.

The use of the ancient symposium in this instance has the effect of:

1. Re-kindling interest by providing a change of pace;
2. Making the atmosphere more congenial;
3. Re-affirming the fact that people have social needs as well as intellectual;
4. Uncovering new ways for shy or timid people to make a contribution to the group.

XIV. Symposium (Modern Concept)

A. What is a symposium (modern concept)?

A symposium is a series of related speeches by 2 to 5 persons qualified to speak with authority on different phases of the same topic or on closely related topics.

The speeches vary in length from 3 to 20 minutes, depending on the number of speeches, the amount of time available, and the topics to be treated. The speakers do not converse with one another; they make presentations to the audience. A chairman is in charge of the symposium.

B. When should this symposium be used?

The symposium is the technique to use when the topic and goals point toward doing one or more of the following:

1. Presenting information in an organized way;
2. Revealing a wide range of authoritative opinion about a controversial topic or issue;
3. Permitting analysis of several related aspects of a controversial topic;
4. Clarifying closely related problems;
5. Assisting people to understand the relationships of various parts of a topic to the topic as a whole;
6. Stimulating fresh thinking by people who tend to have similar interests and background.

C. Who are the personnel involved?

1. *The chairman* presides over the symposium and may direct the arrangements for it. He should have organizing ability and a reasonably good speaking voice. A sense of humor is helpful. He should have enough knowledge about the area to be treated to be able to see that the speeches are interrelated;

2. *The speakers* should be well informed about the topic and capable of making relatively brief, logical presentations that take into account the needs and interests of the audience;

3. *The audience* is usually composed of individuals interested in the topic being discussed. Their intellectual levels and interests will vary considerably. Their presence at the meeting is an indication of some interest.

If controversial issues are involved, many of the persons who make up an audience have made up their minds one way or another before they come to the meeting. Some will know very little, if anything, about the topic under consideration, while others will be informed. The audience may contain persons who do not recognize the existence of a problem or are unable to identify the problem in terms of personal opinions and values. The audience may also include persons who know something about the issues but have reached no conclusions.

D. What is the usual pattern of communication?

During the symposium the talking is done by the chairman and the speakers. The technique is characterized by one-way verbal communication as the diagram on the next page shows:

E. Advantages and limitations of the symposium

1. *Advantages:*

a. The audience has the benefit of a wide range of knowledge, experience, and opinion relating to the topic;

b. Several short speeches tend to stimulate listening and aid learning when it is necessary to impart a considerable amount of information.

c. This technique tends to guard against over-simplification and

176

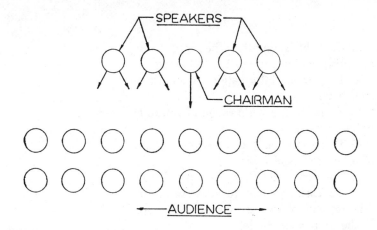

distortion since it requires that various aspects of the topic be covered;

d. Information and opinion can be presented to persons who will not or cannot use printed materials;

e. Taking part in a symposium can have the effect of encouraging each speaker to carefully prepare his speech and stay on the topic.

2. *Limitations:*

a. The audience has no opportunity for active participation;

b. An overly long symposium can be boring and tiring;

c. It is difficult to determine the effects of the speeches on the audience;

d. It is not always possible to obtain enough competent speakers to cover adequately each important aspect of the topic.

F. *Check list for appraising the symposium as a choice of technique*

This list can be used in making the final decision as to whether or not the symposium (modern concept) is the most appropriate technique to use for a particular adult learning situation. If the answers tend to be "no" or "undecided," consider using another technique.

	Yes	No	Unde-cided

1. Can the symposium be used to accomplish one or more of the following:

a. To present information in an organized way?

b. To present a wide range of informed opinion?

c. To permit analyses of several phases of a controversial topic?

d. To clarify closely related problems?

e. To assist people to understand the relationships of various phases of the topic to the topic as a whole?

f. To stimulate thinking in a one-interest group?

2. Do we have clear-cut goals to achieve?

3. Are we reasonably certain that verbal participation by the audience is not essential at this point in the program?

4. Do we have available for each speech a person with these qualifications:

a. Knowledge of the topic?

b. Ability to use words and examples that the audience understands?

c. Ability to make an organized presentation?

d. Ability to stay within the time limit?

e. Willingness to speak to the needs and interests of the audience?

5. Can we:

a. Provide the necessary physical set-up?

b. Insure audience comfort?

6. Do we have available a chairman who can:

a. Plan with the speakers and carefully instruct them?

b. Introduce the symposium and each
speaker effectively?   ___ ___ ___

c. Relate each speech to the topic and
goals?   ___ ___ ___

d. See that each speaker stays within the
time limit?   ___ ___ ___

e. Encourage thoughtful listening and
follow-up study?   ___ ___ ___

7. Are there other techniques that might
be more appropriate choices?   ___ ___ ___

If yes, what are they and why? _____

_____

_____

G. Responsibilities of the personnel involved in the symposium

1. *What does the chairman do?*

a. *Prior to the meeting,* the chairman:

(1) Plans for proper physical arrangements and audience comfort;

(2) Tries to understand the topic and the goals;

(3) Studies the symposium;

(4) Reflects about the characteristics of the group that is anticipated. He asks himself, "What do I know about the age, sex, background, and points of view of the audience? What will they have in common? In what respects will their interest in and knowledge about the topic vary?" He also considers the implications of all this for instructing the speakers and conducting the symposium;

(5) Gets acquainted with the speakers so that he can introduce them, explaining the following to them:

(a) The topic and the desired goals,

(b) The relationship of each speech to the others,

(c) The relationship of the symposium to other parts of the series, if more than one meeting is planned,

(d) The order of the presentations and the length of each,

(e) The needs, interests, and characteristics of the expected audience,

(f) Whether or not the speakers are requested to submit written copies of their speeches;

(6) Learns about each speaker's plans for using educational aids and his preferences in the use of a lectern and a public address system;

(7) Explores the possibilities of encouraging advanced preparation and study by the audience;

(8) Prepares an introduction that will make clear:

(a) The topic and goals for the symposium and their importance,

(b) The topic to be covered in each speech and what the listener can hope to gain from each,

(c) The name, title, background, and qualifications of each speaker,

(d) The relationships between each speech (and the symposium) and parts of the program which may have preceded each or which may follow,

(e) The intended length of each speech,

(f) The responsibilities of the audience (For example, are they to write down questions or comments to be used later in a forum or question period?).

b. *During the symposium,* the chairman:

(1) Presents the introduction he has prepared (see above) with enthusiasm and cordiality, usually making a brief identification of the speakers during his main introduction; then, as he introduces each speech, he gives details about the title, background, and qualifications of the speaker;

(2) Sees that each speech starts and ends on schedule. He may devise a way to tactfully warn the speaker as he approaches his time limit; one way is to hold up a card to attract the speaker's attention;

(3) Makes one or two appropriate remarks at the close of each speech. In these remarks, which are intended to promote learning, the chairman may point up issues or raise questions for the audience to think about;

180

(4) Provides continuity from one speech to the next and stresses the relationships among the speeches.

c. *After the speeches have been completed,* the chairman:

(1) Makes some appropriate concluding remarks, thanking the speakers, suggesting follow-up study and action to the audience and relating the symposium to the goals of the meeting or series as a whole;

(2) Makes a final summary, if it has been agreed that one will be given, or names another person to do it;

(3) Closes the meeting or turns over its control to the appropriate person.

2. *What do the speakers do?*

a. *Prior to the meeting,* the speakers:

(1) Plan their speeches with the needs and interests of the audience in mind;

(2) Plan to use ideas, vocabulary, and examples appropriate to the background and experience of the audience;

(3) Plan to use appropriate educational aids if desired;

(4) Try to understand the relationships of the speeches to each other (The speakers may assist the chairman in clarifying these relationships.);

(5) Plan to stay within the time allotted for each speech;

(6) If they agree to submit a written draft of their speeches, they should meet the deadline for this obligation.

b. *During the symposium,* the speakers:

(1) Make logical and organized presentations;

(2) Use suitable vocabulary and helpful examples;

(3) Stay within the allotted time limit;

(4) Constantly observe audience reaction, in an effort to make their speeches as meaningful as possible;

(5) Try to keep in mind that they are not only "telling people" but seeking to enable learning to take place.

3. *What is expected of the audience?*

a. *Prior to the symposium,* the audience member:

(1) Prepares by reading appropriate materials and thinking about the topic to be treated;

(2) Tries to understand the goals the symposium is to achieve and the goals of the meeting or series;

b. *During and after the symposium,* the audience member:

(1) Listens carefully to each speech;
(2) Tries to relate the speech to his own experience;
(3) Keeps in mind the goals of the symposium;
(4) Undertakes appropriate follow-up study and action.

H. Physical arrangements and audience comfort

1. *Physical set-up.*

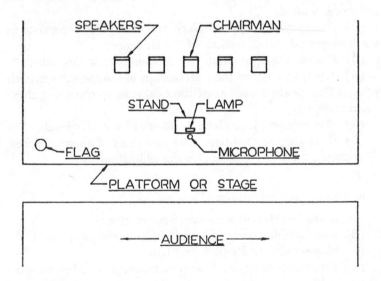

2. *Audience comfort.* Keep the following points in mind when making arrangements:

a. Extremes in temperature are distracting;

b. The audience must be comfortably seated with no one facing a glaring light;

c. The audience must be able to see and hear the chairman and the speakers;

d. Select a room or auditorium appropriate to the size of the group and the character of the meeting;

e. Provide a platform or stage if necessary;

f. Provide chairs and table(s) on the platform or stage to accommodate the chairman and speakers and a lectern if the speakers would like to use one;

g. Secure a public address system with individual microphones for each speaker, if necessary; be certain to check its operation carefully prior to the meeting;

h. Make arrangements for the effective use of any educational aids that the speakers intend to use. Check for the location and proper functioning of electrical outlets, if aids requiring electricity are to be used. Plan to remove the educational aids from view after their use.

I. How to evaluate after the symposium (modern concept) has been conducted

The following check list will aid in appraising how effectively this technique has been conducted. It is for the use of (1) the persons who selected the symposium as the appropriate technique and (2) those present during the symposium.

It may be desirable to have mimeographed or dittoed copies of the check list available for use after the symposium.

If the replies tend to be "no" and "undecided," the symposium probably has been used ineffectively; future errors can be avoided if the various replies are discussed briefly in a cooperative way.

	Yes	No	Unde-cided
1. Was the topic appropriate:			
a. For the audience?	___	___	___
b. To the technique?	___	___	___
2. Was each speaker's presentation:			
a. Well organized?	___	___	___
b. Understandable by the audience?	___	___	___

c. Related to the interests and needs of the audience?   ___ ___ ___

d. Suited to the goals?   ___ ___ ___

e. Confined to his assignment?   ___ ___ ___

3. Were appropriate educational aids employed?   ___ ___ ___

4. Were educational aids used effectively?   ___ ___ ___

5. Was the physical set-up suitable for the effective use of this technique?   ___ ___ ___

6. Was audience comfort adequately provided for?   ___ ___ ___

7. Did the chairman:

a. Successfully instruct all speakers?   ___ ___ ___

b. Make an effective introduction to the symposium and each speaker?   ___ ___ ___

c. Include all the necessary information in his introduction?   ___ ___ ___

d. Encourage the audience to listen carefully?   ___ ___ ___

e. Relate the speeches to the topic and goals for the meeting or series as a whole?   ___ ___ ___

f. See to it that each speaker stayed within his time limit?   ___ ___ ___

g. Encourage appropriate follow-up study and action?   ___ ___ ___

8. Did the audience members:

a. Make advanced preparation?   ___ ___ ___

b. Listen with interest?   ___ ___ ___

c. Appear to understand and learn from the presentations?   ___ ___ ___

d. Appear willing to undertake follow-up study and action?   ___ ___ ___

9. Were there times during the symposium when audience participation seemed desirable?   ___ ___ ___

10. What was accomplished:

a. Were worthwhile points made?   ___ ___ ___

184

b. Did audience members apparently acquire new information, viewpoints, or attitudes?

_____ _____ _____

c. Did the presentation relate to the goals?

_____ _____ _____

d. Have problems or needs emerged which point toward further study or action? _____ _____ _____

e. Was there evidence of willingness to accept responsibility for further study or action?

_____ _____ _____

11. Was the symposium an appropriate technique for this situation?

_____ _____ _____

What other techniques might have been effective and why? _____

_____

_____

J. How the symposium might be used—an example

A state association of adult educators is holding its annual convention for about 150 members. At one of the general sessions, they will treat the topic "Current Trends in Five Major Areas of Adult Education." At least one qualified resource person is available for each of the following areas:

(1) public school adult education, (2) library adult education, (3) labor education, (4) rural adult education, and (5) adult religious education.

A panel discussion would not be appropriate since the purpose of the presentation is to offer systematically new information to the audience rather than to discuss issues or problems. A symposium (modern concept) is selected, with each speaker to be allowed 15 minutes. Each speech will be on a specific phase of the main topic.

In this instance, the symposium is superior to a single long speech covering all aspects of the topic because (1) no single speaker is qualified to cover all phases of the topic and (2) several short presentations should help to hold the interest of the audience.

One problem presents itself: the speakers will be well-known experts who are accustomed to speaking with authority. It may therefore be difficult for a chairman to hold each speaker to his allotted 15 minutes. Therefore, a chairman is selected who has status and reputation comparable to that of the speakers. It is hoped that he will be able to keep the speeches on schedule without giving any speaker cause to be offended.

CHAPTER 4

Six Subtechniques

The subtechnique, as described in this book, resembles a technique but is less complex and functions for a shorter period of time. A subtechnique is used to adapt a technique to the requirements of a particular teaching-learning situation. It cannot serve as the main procedure for a learning situation. A colloquy might be the only technique used in a one-and-one-half-hour meeting, but such a subtechnique as a buzz session or audience reaction team cannot function in this manner. It supplements one or more techniques, which carry the main procedural load for the learning situation.

With the exception of the question period and idea inventory, the subtechniques explained in this chapter are usually used with groups in excess of 30 persons. They are most frequently used with groups having from 50 to 500 persons.

As with techniques, it is important to avoid using subtechniques without giving thought to their purpose and function. There should be sound educational reason for the choice of any subtechnique that is used. One subtechnique that is frequently used carelessly is the buzz session. It is not uncommon to see buzz sessions used for no particular purpose. A chairman will say, "Now we are going to divide into buzz groups." This sounds rather progressive. The buzz groups are told to go ahead and discuss. After a time, the buzz sessions are ended and no one discovers what was supposed to have been accomplished by the use of this procedure.

Similarly with the question period. Often a speech is followed by a question period for no apparent reason. The chairman will say "Are there any questions?" and a painful silence may ensue. This subtechnique requires careful preparation and handling for effective results.

Following are six sub-techniques which, when used appropriately, can be helpful.

I. AUDIENCE REACTION TEAM

A. *What is an audience reaction team?*

This subtechnique uses three to five audience representatives who interrupt a speaker, or other resource person, at appropriate times to seek immediate clarification of points that seem obscure, or to assist the speaker in treating the needs of the audience.

Examples:

1. An expert on investments is to speak to an audience of interested citizens who know very little about the subject. It will be necessary for the speaker to introduce a specialized vocabulary and some concepts which he regards as elementary. To guard against misunderstanding and try to insure that the audience does not get lost during the speech, an audience reaction team is used to interrupt whenever they feel that their questions or comments will promote learning.

2. A laboratory technician is to demonstrate a new piece of equipment to a rather large group of hospital board members who are taking part in an institute. The purpose of the demonstration is to show the complexity of modern equipment and to promote understanding of the cost of medical care. It is expected that the demonstration will involve the use of terms which are unfamiliar to the lay persons who make up the audience. So an audience reaction team is assigned the task of asking questions during the demonstration at the points where clarification seems necessary.

B. *What are the uses of this subtechnique?*

1. The audience reaction team is based on the idea that:

a. Speakers or resource persons sometimes are not understood and go on talking over the heads of the listeners or explaining something that the audience already understands;

b. Three to five audience representatives will ask for clarification at much the same points as the audience would, if it were practical to allow the audience to interrupt at will.

188

2. This subtechnique is used:

a. When the subject matter is likely to be difficult to understand;

b. When the resource persons welcome interruption in the interest of adequate learning;

c. When the audience is so large that interruptions from all audience members might be impractical or annoying;

d. With these techniques *only:* speech, modern symposium, demonstration, or the interview.

C. How to use audience reaction teams

1. *Prior to the meeting:*

a. The chairman explains this subtechnique to the speaker or other resource persons who are to treat the assigned topic:

b. If the speaker approves the use of audience reaction teams, the chairman selects a group of three to five representative audience members in advance and instructs them regarding their task. When instructing them, he makes clear:

(1) Where they are to sit on the platform;

(2) Whether or not microphones will be used;

(3) The general nature of questions and comments that will be appropriate;

(4) Their responsibility to ask helpful questions that will assist the audience to learn. (They should be requested not to use the occasion as an opportunity to show off their knowledge or annoy the speaker in any way.)

2. *During the meeting:*

a. The chairman or moderator introduces the topic and technique (which may be a speech, symposium, or demonstration, etc.) and explains to the audience how the reaction team functions and the reasons for using it;

b. The members of the audience reaction team interrupt whenever they feel the need of clarification of ideas, a definition of a term, or an example;

c. When the presentation is ended, the members of the reaction team return to their places in the audience.

D. Advantages of this subtechnique when it is properly used

1. It becomes possible to make use of a speaker or resource person who otherwise might fail to communicate effectively to the audience;

2. Seeing the audience reaction team act as their representatives can stimulate interest among the audience members;

3. The persons who serve on the audience reaction team have an opportunity to gain experience before an audience and gain insight into the problems of communicating clearly;

4. The speaker often gains insight into his own limitations as a communicator of information.

E. Some suggestions

1. Do not select as members of the audience reaction team persons who are overly aggressive or prone to show off before an audience, or persons too timid to do the job asked of them;

2. Use this subtechnique with the speech, modern symposium, demonstration, or the interview;

3. Be sure that the person to be interrupted consents to the use of this subtechnique.

F. Diagram of audience reaction team

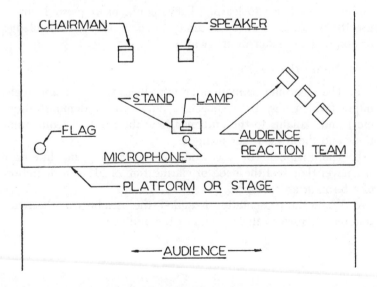

II. Buzz Session

A. *What is a buzz session?*

A buzz session—an audience divided into several small groups, meeting simultaneously, to discuss a topic or perform a task assigned them.

The small groups (buzz groups) meet for a relatively short time and for uncomplex purposes—such as developing one or two questions to put to a speaker.

Examples:

1. If a group of 200 or 300 persons wished to discuss some particular problem, understand an issue, or express their wishes for action to their officers or a committee, it would be quite difficult short of voting. In voting the issues to be voted upon are often oversimplified in that the large body of voters have little opportunity to present their true opinions. If, however, a group of several hundred persons can be divided into a dozen face-to-face discussion groups, each group can talk about the issue for 10 or 20 minutes. Then one of the members of each group can report for about two minutes to the larger body. This enables the opinions of the total body to be more accurately discerned.

2. A speaker has agreed to talk to a group of local labor union leaders on the topic "Overcoming Member Apathy." Since he feels (a) that the audience is part of the problem and (b) that he is not clear as to all the ways in which apathy expresses itself in labor unions, he precedes his talk by a buzz session. One half of the buzz groups are asked to identify ways in which union members are apathetic, while the other half are to suggest causes of apathy. In each buzz group a recorder writes down the points brought out in the discussion. Then the audience takes a short break (intermission) while the speaker reads over the recorders' notes and builds his speech around the suggestions that have come from the buzz groups. In this instance, using buzz sessions should enable the speaker to:

a. Involve the audience in the learning experience in such a way that they begin to see themselves as part of the problem;

191

b. Show that he is as concerned with the way the audience sees the problem as he is with his own interpretation of it.

B. *What are the uses of this subtechnique?*

This subtechnique can be used for one or more of the following purposes:

1. To permit discussion, even though the group is a large one;
2. To identify needs and interests which a learning group wishes to have treated;
3. To obtain the contributions of persons who, for one reason or another, will not speak up in the presence of a large group;
4. To enable a large audience to help evaluate a learning experience—that is, suggestions for improving the meeting can be developed in buzz groups.

C. *How to conduct a buzz session*

The meeting chairman or another person responsible for the buzz session does the following:

1. *Prior to the meeting,* the chairman:

a. Makes sure that he knows the purpose of the buzz session to be conducted;

b. Clarifies the task of each buzz group. Is each group to do the same thing? Are the groups to raise one or more questions, agree on one or more disadvantages, make two suggestions, etc.;

c. Develops a general plan for leadership. Are the buzz groups to (1) be assigned leaders, (2) choose their own leaders, or (3) operate without leaders? (The latter procedure is not recommended unless very small groups of well-trained and self-disciplined persons are involved.) Who will speak for each group, or are written reports to be handed in? Will a recorder and a leader be used? Should the recorders be appointed in advance?

d. Visits the meeting place and examines the facilities. He considers how the audience will be divided and where each buzz group will meet;

e. Develops his final plan for organizing the buzz session. This includes:

(1) How the leadership will be chosen and instructed;

(2) How the audience will be divided and buzz groups established (by counting off or handing out colored cards, for example*);

(3) The instructions to be given each buzz group about its task and how to proceed;

(4) How to make use of the contributions of each buzz group (who will report to the total group and how);

(5) Instructions which are prepared and distributed to the audience (or the leaders only).

2. *During the meeting,* the chairman:

a. Explains the purpose of the buzz session and how the audience is to be divided, asking the audience not to begin discussion immediately after groups are formed.

b. Helps to divide the audience into groups of about 5 to 15 persons, the group members facing each other in a circle;

c. Suggests that group members spend a minute or two to get acquainted with each other;

d. Sees that each group appoints a leader and a recorder;

e. Restates the assignment—exactly what each group is expected to do and the length of time for discussion (about 10 to 20 minutes depending on the circumstances);

f. Keeps the assignment simple—"develop one question," or "agree on one disadvantage," or "make two suggestions";

g. Instructs the groups to begin discussion and cautions them about allowing one or two persons to dominate the discussion;

h. Gives a warning two minutes prior to ending the discussion;

i. Stops the discussion and reassembles the audience;

j. Allows the recorders a moment to edit or re-write the contributions of their respective groups;

k. Has leaders or recorders report their contributions to the total group (unless other plans have been made to make use of these contributions).

---

* Each person receives a colored card when he registers or enters the room. He joins all the other persons holding the card of the same color at the time and place designated by the chairman.

D. What are the advantages of this subtechnique when it is properly used?

1. A relatively large number of ideas, questions, or recommendations can be obtained in a very short time;

2. Every one involved in the meeting has a good opportunity for verbal participation;

3. The group can express needs and interests that it wishes to see covered, thus helping the speaker or other resource person to learn what to treat in their presentations.

E. Some suggestions

1. Don't try to use this subtechnique for complex learning purposes—the assignment should always be a simple one;

2. Avoid allowing the discussion to extend beyond 20 minutes;

3. Inform the audience about the possibility of the danger of domination of the discussion by one or two persons in the buzz group;

4. Because misunderstanding of the assignment is common, repeat instructions several times if necessary; sometimes it helps to have the instructions and assignment mimeographed for distribution to the participants;

5. Plan to avoid confusion when the audience divides into buzz groups. Leaders for each group can be appointed in advance, briefed, and an area assigned to each for organizing his group. Sometimes each small group will want to select its own recorder and leader. The choice here would depend on how advanced and disciplined the audience is;

6. Consider physical limitations in advance. For example, this subtechnique will not work in an auditorium with seats fastened to the floor.

F. Diagram of a buzz session

This diagram shows an audience divided into five small groups. All members of each group should sit in a circle face-to-face.

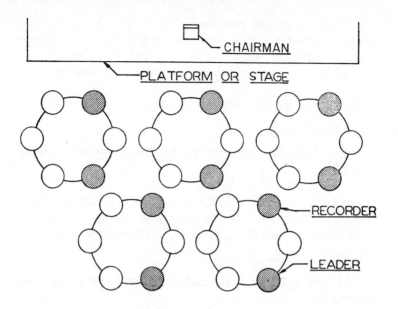

III. Idea Inventory

A. What is the idea inventory?

The idea inventory, sometimes called "brainstorming" or "free-wheeling," is the spontaneous outpouring of ideas pertinent to an area of interest or need about which a group desires to reach a decision. For a limited time (5-15 minutes) ideas are presented freely and are recorded as they are offered without being modified in any way. It is not necessary that ideas be related to each other. During the period of taking inventory, quantity of ideas takes precedence over quality; quality is considered at a later time.

B. What are the uses of this subtechnique?

1. This subtechnique is used:

a. When a group desires to identify several alternative ideas before reaching a basis for making a decision;

b. When many aspects of a problem need to be considered before it can be defined;

195

c. When maximum participation is sought from the entire group. Frequently, persons who are hesitant in offering suggestions will relinquish their restraint when they can present their ideas without feeling compelled to develop or defend them.

C. How to use the idea inventory

1. *Prior to using it:*

a. The chairman explains this subtechnique to the group and suggests:
(1) That a time limit be set;
(2) That a recorder put all ideas on a blackboard as they are presented. (Sometimes it is necessary to use two recorders to avoid slowing down the process or losing contributions.)

2. *While it is being used:*

a. The chairman urges the making of contributions as rapidly as possible;
b. The participants offer ideas:
(1) Without regard to whether or not they will be used later;
(2) Without feeling that they must be related to an idea offered previously;
(3) Without commenting in any way upon the ideas of others.

3. *A suggestion:*

This subtechnique is frequently utilized in connection with group discussion. As an aid in decision-making, it can be put to effective use, for example, by a program planning committee during its initial considerations of possible interest-need-problem areas, topics, and goals.

IV. Listening and Observing Groups

A. What are listening and observing groups?

This subtechnique involves the division of an audience into two or more groups, each of which is assigned specific listening or observing tasks to be performed during a speech, symposium, panel, etc.

196

The purpose of this subtechnique is to promote active listening and observing by each portion of the audience and to assist them to participate effectively during the forum or other educational technique that may follow.

Examples:

1. At a Parent-Teacher's Association meeting, an educator is speaking about "Discipline." One section of the audience listens in terms of the child's point of view, another section listens from the point of view of the teacher, and another from the parent's point of view. Or, groups might be set up in terms of problems, causes, and solutions. Each group might be asked to report its reactions to the total group.

2. During a role-play involving an employer, a shop steward, and an employee, three groups could be set up to observe and listen for factors that account for the behavior of each player. Members of one group observe the role-play with this question in mind: "Why is the employee belligerent?" A second group considers: "What appears to be the employer's attitude toward labor unions?" A third group observes with this question in mind: "How is the shop steward caught between the demands of management and labor?"

B. *What are the uses of this subtechnique?*

Listening and observing groups are used to:

1. Encourage active participation, by means of a specific assignment, in what otherwise might be a passive audience;
2. Help develop ideas and solutions to problems;
3. Set the stage for verbal participation by audience members.

C. *How to use listening and observing groups*

1. *Prior to the meeting:*

a. The persons who are to be involved in the presentation (speech, role-play, demonstration, panel, symposium, etc.) are consulted by the chairman of the meeting regarding the need for listening groups in this particular situation;

b. If it is decided to use listening groups, the chairman works out a plan for dividing the total audience into groups and for using the information and opinions that accumulate in the listening groups. Will the division be made by rows, by sections of the auditorium, or be based on the characteristics of the audience? For example, all parents watch for one factor, all teachers for another;

c. The chairman clarifies what use will be made of the information that becomes available. Will several persons be requested to express ideas or questions? Will the members of each group be asked to write down and hand in questions or observations? Will someone interview a representative of each group in front of the audience? These questions should be answered in relation to the goals and requirements of the particular learning situation.

2. *During the meeting:*

a. The audience is carefully informed about its task, how it is to be divided, and for what purpose;

b. The subject is presented by a speech, role-play, etc.;

c. After the subject is presented, the chairman or moderator takes steps to see that the audience members have an opportunity to participate by giving their ideas or asking questions arising out of their listening and observing groups.

D. Advantages of this subtechnique when it is properly used

1. Active listening and observing are encouraged;

2. Audience members are likely to participate verbally when given the opportunity;

3. Speakers or other persons presenting information are encouraged to clarify their ideas before presenting them;

4. Speakers are encouraged to treat various sides of the subject.

E. Some suggestions

1. Be specific. Vague assignments to the groups will result in confusion;

2. If the audience has very little knowledge concerning the subject being treated, they may be incapable of observing and listening in the necessary way;

3. Be sure that the presentation can be expected to contain the factors for which the members of each group are asked to listen.

F. *Diagram of listening and observing groups*

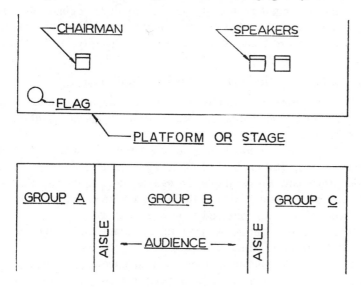

V. QUESTION PERIOD

A. *What is a question period?*

A question period is a 5 to 20-minute portion of a meeting during which audience members ask questions of a speaker or other resource persons.

The question period may be held at almost any point in a program. It can be used before or after a speech, panel, demonstration or similar presentation. It should not be confused with a forum.

Examples:

1. A group views a film that explains the procedure used in preparing a speech. After the film, the group members ask questions of an expert who is thoroughly familiar with the procedure explained in the film;

2. After a group completes a field trip, the participants ask questions of one or more resource persons concerning what they have observed;

3. Some learners are about to explore a topic by means of group discussion. The participants have prepared for the discussion by reading a pamphlet; but before they begin their discussion, they test their understanding of what they have read and secure more facts by questioning an authority on the topic.

B. *What are the uses of this subtechnique?*

1. The question period is used to provide opportunities for the learner to verify that he has understood correctly information presented to him;

2. A question period is used to encourage the learner to test out an interpretation he has made of something that has been said previously. For example, he can say something like this to the resource person: "Would the Korean War be an example of the kind of war you referred to as a limited war?"

3. This subtechnique is used to encourage the audience to request further information;

4. This subtechnique can be used to encourage a group to obtain information or verify facts before carrying on a discussion.

C. *How to use the question period*

1. *Prior to the meeting,* the chairman (or other responsible person):

a. Makes certain that the topic is one that the audience can be expected to have questions about at the point in the program at which the question period is scheduled;

b. Makes certain that the resource person approves of having a question period at the scheduled time;

c. Plans to encourage the asking of questions by the audience members by taking one or more of the following steps:

(1) Informing the audience well in advance that an opportunity for asking questions will be offered;

(2) Providing 3 x 5 cards or scrap paper and pencils for writ-

200

ing down questions during the program that precedes the question period;

(3) Arranging to have the program suspended for two or three minutes at about the half-way point, or immediately prior to the question period itself, so that audience members can ask or write down questions that are fresh in their minds;

d. Decides whether the questions will be asked by the audience members from the floor or collected and read by the chairman or moderator;

e. Arranges to have the questions collected and examined (by a person with knowledge of the topic) before they are asked of the resource person. This is done particularly if the audience is to be larger than 50 persons. This procedure can eliminate duplication and make it possible to group together questions that are related. This procedure is often called screening. Time for screening the questions can be gained by means of a break (intermission), or by going on with another portion of the program;

f. Decides whether or not the chairman will relay the questions to the resource person. If questions come directly from the floor it is usually better to have the chairman relay the questions to the resource person than to have the resource person answer questions directly from the floor. It allows the chairman to restate or repeat a question so that all persons present can hear and understand it;

g. Works out a way of allotting some time to each reply—such as (1) limiting the resource person to one minute per question or (2) taking one question from each category before repeating questions in a particular category;

h. Asks a person or two in advance of the program to ask the first questions in order to get the audience started. Sometimes this form of stimulation may not be necessary.

2. *During the meeting*, the chairman:

a. States the purpose of the question period and the amount of time available;

b. Introduces the person who will attempt to answer the questions;

c. Makes it clear what kind of questions are to be asked;

d. Encourages everyone to participate—making it clear that every person's question is important;

e. Waits patiently if there is a period of silence when he asks for questions;

f. Reads or repeats each question clearly and loudly enough for everyone to hear and understand;

g. Interprets unclear questions to the best of his ability, making certain to acknowledge when he is making such an interpretation;

h. Turns over control of the meeting to the appropriate person at the conclusion of the question period.

D. Advantages of this subtechnique when it is properly used

1. The resource person can identify areas in which he has not been clearly understood by the audience;

2. The learner has an opportunity to request further information, examples, or clarification of something he has seen, read, or heard;

3. If a question occurs to one person in the audience, the chances are good that many others have also thought of it or are interested once it has been raised.

E. Some suggestions

1. Never underestimate the importance of the question period or regard it as easy to conduct. Plan carefully for it and treat it as an important part of the program;

2. Make certain that no one feels that his question is "too silly to ask." The chairman should see, too, that no questioner is embarrassed or permitted to embarrass others;

3. Be sure to allow enough time, if questions are to be collected and screened before they are asked of the resource person.

F. Diagram for a question period

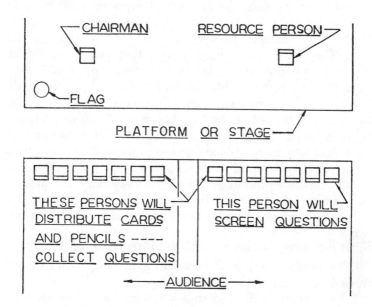

VI. SCREENING PANEL

A. What is the screening panel?

The screening panel is a group of three to five representative members of an audience who discuss with each other the educational needs of the audience they represent in order to reveal this information to a speaker or resource person.

The speaker (or speakers) listen to the discussion, which is carried on in the presence of the audience. While he listens, he develops or adapts the remarks he will make to the audience.

This subtechnique draws its name from its tendency to act as a screen through which the audience's expressed needs and interests filter to the speaker. The panel screens out the important needs to help the speaker or other resource person to treat them during his part of the program.

Example:

At a town meeting, the city school superintendent is to be interviewed on the topic "Expanding Our School Facilities." Most of the audience members are not well-informed on the topic. They have heard various rumors that have been circulating. The superintendent is not certain what aspects of "School Expansion" interest his audience. So it is decided to precede the interview with a screening panel. Since the superintendent is so familiar with his subject and is able to speak without advance preparation, he welcomes the screening panel as a way of gaining insight into the needs and interests of the audience. Listening to the panel made up of its representatives has the effect of (1) stimulating audience interest in the interview and (2) promoting teamwork by demonstrating to the audience members that the superintendent wishes to understand and serve their needs.

B. *What are the uses of this subtechnique?*

1. To permit a resource person to gain insight into the expressed needs and interests of a group;

2. To encourage the audience members to express their interests;

3. To actively involve the entire audience in thought and discussion concerning the topic;

4. To be used for the most part prior to presentations made by means of the following techniques: the interview, the speech, the (modern) symposium, or the panel.

C. *How to use the screening panel*

1. *Prior to the meeting:*

a. The chairman explains the functioning of the screening panel to the speaker or other resource person and asks his permission to use it;

b. If the speaker approves the use of a screening panel, the chairman carefully selects three to five persons who are willing to be members of the screening panel. They should be persons who can converse naturally before an audience without straying from the topic. To these persons he explains:

204

(1) The purpose for using this subtechnique;

(2) Where the screening panel is to sit on the platform;

(3) How long the panel is to carry on its discussion;

(4) Who will act as moderator. (Often no moderator is used because the panel discussion lasts only 10-15 minutes and the panel members are chosen for their ability to converse effectively before an audience.) The meeting chairman or another qualified person may serve as moderator of the panel if leadership seems necessary;

(5) The need for speaking clearly and distinctly since they will be making their contributions for the entire audience to hear.

2. *During the meeting:*

a. The chairman explains the nature and purpose of the screening panel;

b. The chairman calls the panel members to the platform, seats them appropriately for a panel discussion, and introduces them to the audience;

c. The panel members then converse in loud and clear voices about the needs they believe the speaker should treat during his portion of the program;

d. While the speaker listens to the panel discussion, he plans his presentation or adapts it to what he hears.

D. Advantages of this subtechnique when it is properly used

1. The audience members have visible proof that the program was designed to meet their needs and interests;

2. The speaker is encouraged to present only useful, relevant ideas and opinions.

E. Some suggestions

1. The screening panel is usually used prior to the following educational techniques: speech, interview, modern symposium, or panel;

2. Avoid allowing the panel discussion to extend beyond 15 minutes;

3. Provide microphones for the panel if necessary (one microphone for each panel member). The public address equipment should be tested to see that it works properly—not using it is usually preferable to distracting the audience with the efforts of repair men;

4. Be sure to secure the speaker's permission before using this subtechnique.

F. Diagram of the screening panel

After the small groups have concluded their discussion, the panel members take their place before the audience as shown here.

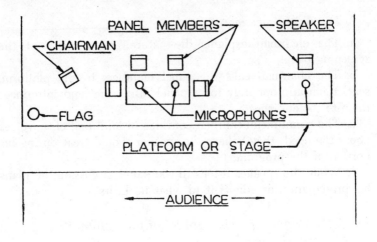

CHAPTER 5

Some Educational Aids

Educational aids differ clearly from techniques and subtechniques. The latter involve a *process* of interaction among people in a group learning situation. Techniques are ways of structuring the teaching-learning situation. Aids, on the other hand, represent *resources*, from which individuals or groups can acquire information. Aids are materials that can be used either at a meeting or for individual study at home. Their use usually helps learning by actively involving one or more of the learner's senses—such as the eye or ear—in a way that supplements or re-enforces what is presented or discussed in the group learning situation.*

I. THE ANNOTATED READING LIST

A. *What is the annotated reading list?*

Reading lists, or bibliographies, are lists of books, articles, and pamphlets that contain useful information about a particular subject that is being studied. An annotated reading list is one in which each item is briefly described. Annotating a reading list increases the chances that an adult will select and read some of the references contained in it.

Examples:

1. On page 237 of this book you will find an annotated reading list which describes books dealing with adult education procedures.

2. A men's club is to hear a talk on "city planning." The program chairman asks the public library to prepare a short anno-

---

* Books and pamphlets are not included because we assume that their use is so common as to call for no explanation or comment. It is worth remembering, however, that any books or pamphlets used should be (1) appropriate as to content—that is, related to the topics and goals for the meeting, (2) on the reading level of the persons who will use them, and (3) printed in large enough type to be read without difficulty.

tated reading list on this topic. The librarian includes only materials that are available in the local library or from bookstores and newstands. She selects interesting articles and books and describes them in such a way as to stimulate interest in reading them. When the list is completed, the program chairman has it duplicated for distribution following the speech. He sends a copy to the speaker and suggests that the speaker refer to items on the reading list during his talk and encourage the audience to do follow-up reading.

B. *Who should obtain or prepare the annotated reading list?*

1. Someone in the learning group can be asked to prepare one;

2. A member of a planning committee can assume this responsibility;

3. The planning committee can request one from a speaker, panel member, or other resource person involved in the meeting program.

C. *Where may annotated reading lists be obtained?*

1. Many books and articles contain ready-made reading lists;

2. Public schools, colleges, and public libraries are logical sources. Many churches, hospitals, and industries, as well as national organizations have libraries that can assist with the task. Some state and county organizations like P.T.A. and the larger Community Councils have special collections of materials and reading lists;

3. Some universities have special agencies or bureaus which assist people with tasks of this kind.

D. *Some Suggestions*

1. An annotated reading list should not be so long as to be overwhelming—10-20 carefully selected and appropriate titles are usually enough;

2. In preparing the list, strive for accuracy and initiating of interest;

3. Begin preparation far enough in advance so as to have the list available in quantity with enough time to plan for its effective use;

208

4. Refer to the list several times during the meeting. Encourage people to use it and explain where the items on the list are to be found. Mention the list at subsequent meetings;

5. Never assume that merely passing out a reading list insures that people will read the recommended references. They must be encouraged to do so;

6. Try to give each list an attractive title. Rather than a forbidding phrase like "An Annotated Bibliography," the title might be "Some Useful and Accurate Materials for Further Reading";

7. Consider distributing reading lists several days before the meeting in order to encourage advance study.

II. The Case History

A. *What is a case history?*

A case history is a detailed written report describing an event, incident, or situation that a learning group can profitably analyze and discuss. The case sometimes deals with the behavior of a person or a group. It may be based on an actual incident or an imaginary one. The group members read the case history before the meeting. The case can be discussed or analyzed by means of any of several appropriate techniques: group discussion, panel, colloquy, or symposium. Analysis of the case is usually carried out with the help of an instructor or a resource person who has considerable knowledge of the area from which the case is drawn.

Case histories are used to:

1. Reveal the problems and issues found in a particular situation;

2. Aid in seeking solutions to problems;

3. Enable the learner to consider various interpretations of a situation, an event, or the behavior of a person;

4. Help people to develop analytical skills.

Example:

A committee is planning in-service education activities for 50 adult evening-school teachers. The teachers want assistance with the problem of "Helping the Timid Class Member to Participate."

The committee members know that one teacher in the school has had success in overcoming this problem. They consider asking him to tell the learning group how he does it. But he is not an effective speaker. They consider interviewing him as a way of treating this information. It is suggested that a case history be prepared from an example supplied by this teacher. This case history may include several possible ways of assisting a timid person to participate. Or, it may be limited to a description of a situation with different courses of action to be supplied by the members of the learning group when they discuss the case at the in-service education meeting.

After thoughtful discussion, the planning committee decides that a case history will be helpful for these reasons:

1. It will increase the time available during the meeting for analysis and discussion of the problem by introducing the learner to factual information prior to the meeting;

2. It will make use of the experience and knowledge available from an experienced and successful teacher;

3. The problem to be analyzed is suitable for description in a brief written report.

After deciding to use a case history, the committee still faces the task of selecting learning techniques and subtechniques through which the learning group will be able to analyze and discuss the problem as described in the case history.

Since the group will number 50 persons, it seems wise to break up into smaller groups for at least a part of the time available. The committee finally decides to approach the topic by means of a colloquy to be preceded by buzz groups. The chairman will briefly introduce the topic, then review the case history which has been distributed before the meeting. Then, he will divide the audience into groups of from 6 to 10 persons. These groups will be assigned the task of suggesting ways that the timid person in the case history might be helped to participate. After about 10 minutes the buzz groups will be ended and the colloquy will begin. One person selected from each buzz group will take his place on the platform along with a moderator and one or more resource persons. (In this instance, the resource person will be

210

an expert in adult education processes and procedures.) The audience representatives will present to the resource person the suggestions developed in the buzz groups. He will comment on these suggestions; then the entire group, under the guidance of the moderator, will have opportunities to contribute to a discussion of the topic: "Helping the Timid Class Member to Participate."

B. *How long should the case history be?*

It must be brief yet relatively complete, giving the reader enough information to permit thoughtful analysis and discussion. Depending on the complexity of the situation described, it may run from 500 to 3,000 words. It usually describes what is known of the background or history of the situation and the situation itself. It may include possible courses of action or questions for discussion.

C. *Where to obtain case histories*

1. Ask a qualified person to write one;
2. Secure them from books or pamphlets found in libraries;
3. Request them from district or national headquarters of various organizations and agencies.

D. *Some suggestions*

1. Use only case histories that have enough information to permit analysis at the meeting;
2. Use a case history that is realistic, practical, and within the knowledge and interests of the persons attending;
3. Be sure to get the case history in the hands of the learner in ample time for him to read it carefully before it is analyzed and discussed;
4. Select the best techniques and subtechniques for analyzing and discussing the case history during the meeting. When the group is large, these techniques and subtechniques are most likely to be used: panel-forum, symposium-forum, speech-forum, interview-forum, colloquy, and buzz sessions. For smaller groups, group discussion can be used.

III. The Exhibit

A. *What is an exhibit?*

An exhibit is a collection of related materials put on display to aid learning. Reading materials, farm produce, manufactured products, individual projects, and natural science collections are among the things that are commonly exhibited. The exhibit should provide the learner with accurate, concrete illustrations. It can include actual examples of the subject or be based on photos, illustrations, and diagrams.

Examples:

1. A women's organization is devoting a series of programs to politics and government in Latin-American countries. Each meeting deals with a different nation. The planning committee decides to use two exhibits at each meeting. One will be designed to picture the way of life in the country under study. It will show living conditions and customs. The other exhibit will be designed to illustrate politics and government in the country under study. The exhibits will include books, photos, charts, and products contributed by members of the organization.

2. A state association for adult education devoted its annual convention to the topic "Current Trends in Adult Education." Four major phases of adult education were emphasized: public schools, libraries, churches, and university extension. Four speakers described trends in these adult education areas. Each exhibit illustrated and supplemented some of the ideas treated by each speaker.

Each exhibit was developed by a person specializing in the area of adult education to be illustrated. An exhibits chairman worked with these persons to make certain that the exhibits were in line with the topics and goals of the planning committee. The exhibits chairman also saw to it that the person doing each exhibit knew what points would be made by the speaker dealing with his area. For example, the exhibits chairman found out what trends in adult education in churches the speaker intended to describe to the audience. He passed this information on so that this particular exhibit would show some of those trends.

212

During the program (at the convention), the chairman encouraged thoughtful viewing of the exhibits: after the first two speeches, the chairman gave the audience members 20 minutes to view the exhibits. Then he reassembled them to hear the other two speeches.

B. Who develops the exhibit?

1. A qualified person within the organization or learning group itself may be asked to be responsible for an exhibit;

2. A member of the planning committee can assume this task;

3. An educational agency may agree to provide one. Many organizations have ready-made exhibits that are available for loan. (For example, the Red Cross, the Heart Foundation, and the Senate Commission on Alcoholism.) A library may be willing to develop an exhibit or assist the person who is doing it.

C. What are criteria for a good educational exhibit?

1. *Unity and cohesion.* The exhibit does not try to do everything. Some aspects should be selected for emphasis and tied together by a theme;

2. *Attractiveness.* A neat, appealing presentation is essential;

3. *Appeal to the senses.* The proper use of color, light, and the use of three dimensions can enable the exhibit to have impact on the senses of the viewer. Sound can sometimes be used;

4. *Good location.* The exhibit should be placed where it shows to good advantage and where the viewer can take whatever time he needs to examine it.

D. Some suggestions

1. Begin planning the exhibit well in advance of its intended use;

2. For meetings using several exhibits, appoint an exhibits chairman to work with the persons preparing each exhibit;

3. Take the size of exhibits into account when selecting display rooms. Make certain there will be ample space for the exhibits if they are to be displayed in the room where meetings will be held. Often exhibits are placed in rooms set aside specifically for them;

4. Have a clear-cut *educational* purpose for each exhibit. The exhibit should be clearly related to the total program;

5. Encourage serious viewing of exhibits by setting aside time for the group to examine them;

6. It is often desirable to station a person at each exhibit to answer questions;

7. In designing exhibits:

a. Begin with the purpose or goal of the exhibit;

b. Consider the needs, interests, and educational background of the viewer;

c. Use colored pins, colored pictures and paper, colored lights, animation, and sound (if appropriate);

d. Use moving parts, if possible;

8. Some suggestions for further reading:

Dale, Edgar, and East, Marjorie. *Display for Learning*. New York: Dryden Press, 1952;

Brown, James W., et al. *Audio-Visual Instruction Materials and Methods*. New York: McGraw-Hill, 1959.

IV. Films, Filmstrips, and Slides

A. *What are the characteristics of these audio-visual aids?*

A filmstrip is a series of still pictures with captions, in sequential order, on 35mm film with sprocket holes on each side. These are shown on a screen or light colored wall by a projector designed for this purpose. Sometimes a narration accompanies the filmstrips and is presented by an amplifying unit designed for that purpose.

A set of 2 x 2 inch slides used with a slide projector and screen is often effectively used.

The film commonly used for educational purposes is a 16mm (black and white or color) sound or silent film that runs from 10-40 minutes. It requires a 16mm sound projector, a screen, and a qualified operator.

Filmstrips and slides are much less expensive than films. The person using filmstrips and slides has a great deal of flexibility. He can stop the presentation, back up, repeat, and skip items in a way that is impossible with films. Also, it is not difficult to make slides as they are needed, while producing a film is beyond the resources of most groups.

All of these audio-visual aids are useful to:

1. Present information;
2. Help teach procedures;
3. Raise issues;
4. Provide the viewers with a common experience that can be built upon through discussion or other kinds of programs;
5. Introduce a problem or topic and stimulate interest in further learning;
6. Help the learner to integrate and tie together what he has learned;
7. Stimulate further study.

Examples:

1. A group of 20 adults is using a study course on "Great Issues in American History." One session is scheduled to be devoted to "Slavery." Two months prior to this meeting, the leader asks if anyone in the group would be interested in investigating what films, filmstrips, and slides are available on this topic. One woman agrees to do so. She goes to the public library, where she examines several catalogues listing the audio-visual aids. She finds several films and several filmstrips that seem to offer possibilities. A librarian helps her to find where these aids are available and their cost of rental. She writes a brief summary of each and types up copies of her description for use by members of her group. At the next meeting of the study group, the leader asks her to report on her progress. She distributes copies of the summary that she has prepared. The leader reminds the group of the suggested topics and goals for the session on "Slavery." The group eliminates several films and slides which clearly are not appropriate. Another group member volunteers to preview several aids that seem most promising. Previewing narrows the choice down to one film and one filmstrip that are appropriate and available for use on the desired dates. It is decided to use the film because it: (1) is the more timely of the two, (2) raises issues for discussion which are in line with those recommended in the study course, and (3) seems suited for an adult group while the filmstrip is clearly aimed at high school students.

2. A committee is planning a neighborhood meeting for a large audience on the problem "The Future Growth of Our Community." One topic which they wish to cover is "Advantages and Disadvantages of Securing New Industry for Our Community." They investigate what films, filmstrips, and slides are available. After careful evaluation they narrow the choice to two:

a. A film distributed at no cost by a Chamber of Commerce which urges the viewer to actively seek new industry;

b. A filmstrip that objectively presents several points of view about this issue.

Several committee members urge the use of the film because it is attractively produced in color and has sound accompanying it which the filmstrip lacks. A businessman strongly supports the use of the film, also, because he has made up his mind that securing new industry is one way for his community to grow.

The committee chairman suggests that the committee go back and review the goals they have set for their meeting. One goal is "to present various sides of controversial issues." Another goal is "to show that cultural and social growth are as important as industrial growth." Once they have reminded themselves of these goals, the committee members quickly reject the film, with its thinly veiled propaganda, in favor of the filmstrip that objectively presents several points of view about the issue.

B. What are criteria for selecting these audio-visual aids?

It is important to use films, filmstrips, and slides only when they are the most appropriate resources for learning. Too often they are used merely because they happen to be available or because someone suggests that their use would enliven the meeting, or someone wants to have a show. These are not good reasons for selecting any resources. Selection of films, filmstrips, and slides should be based on these factors:

1. *Topics, goals, and purposes.* Does the educational aid present useful information? Does it raise issues that the group can profitably discuss? Is its content appropriate for the purposes and goals of the meeting?

2. *Accuracy and timeliness.* Is the educational aid accurate

216

and unbiased? Has it become out-of-date to an extent that is distracting?

3. *Educational level*. Is the educational aid appropriate for the expected audience as regards vocabulary, the examples that are used, and over-all point of view?

4. *Availability*. Is the educational aid available for the time it is to be used and at a reasonable cost? Are adequate viewing facilities, equipment, and a qualified projectionist available?

C. Where to get films and help in selecting them

You can get films and assistance from these sources:

1. County and city public school audio-visual coordinators;
2. Public libraries;
3. Commercial sources—many large corporations have films available for free or rental distribution;
4. Non-profit agencies—foundations, national education, health, and welfare agencies;
5. Government agencies—U.S. Office of Education's Office of Visual Education issues occasional film lists on special subjects;
6. College and university film rental libraries.

D. Some catalogues and reference books that may be useful

Bluebook of Audio-Visual Materials. Chicago: Educational Screen and Audio-Visual Guide;

Brown, James W., et al. *A.V. Instructional Materials and Methods.* New York: McGraw-Hill, 1959;

A *Directory of 16mm Film Libraries.* Washington, D.C.: U.S. Office of Education;

Educators Guide to Free Films. Randolph, Wisconsin: Educator's Progress Service;

Educators Guide to Free Filmstrips. Randolph, Wisconsin: Educator's Progress Service.

E. Steps in using these educational aids

Once you have decided that the use of films, filmstrips, or slides may be appropriate for a learning situation, you are ready to take these steps:

217

1. *Prior to the meeting:*

a. Examine catalogues describing what is available;

b. Select and order for previewing the educational aids that seem most appropriate;

c. Preview the educational aids:

(1) Check each aid against the criteria for selection (see B, above);

(2) Take notes that will be useful in introducing it;

(3) Note issues and questions for discussion;

d. If it is decided that a film, filmstrip, or slides is appropriate for the learning activity, reserve it for use at the proper time;

e. Arrange for the facilities, equipment, and operator that will be needed for the showing (Don't forget screen, extension cords, spare bulbs, and take-up reels of the proper size.);

f. If desirable, reproduce in quantity, for distribution at the meeting, the important points, steps, or issues found in the educational aids to be used;

g. Prepare to introduce the educational aid, by mentioning its purpose, title, and special feature to watch for. It may be necessary to define or explain some terms or ideas that are likely to present difficulties for the viewer.

2. *During the meeting:*

a. Pre-check all physical factors: electrical outlet (Will it operate when the lights are out?), position of projector, operating condition of projector, the procedure for darkening the room;

b. Thread and focus the projector (testing the sound, if sound is involved);

c. Give the introduction (see g, above);

d. Show the film, filmstrip, or slides:

(1) You can show all or part;

(2) You can stop for questions and clarification;

(3) You can repeat all or part;

e. Follow the presentation with an appropriate educational technique or subtechnique for discussing or reacting to it.

V. The Information Brief

A. *What is an information brief?*

This educational aid consists of from one to three pages of specific information about a topic to be considered at a meeting. The brief usually divides the topic into several main areas in the manner of an outline. Under each heading are contained useful facts along with brief quotations from reliable sources. Briefs are usually mimeographed and distributed, in advance of the meeting if possible, to all persons who plan to attend.

By carefully reading the brief prior to the meeting or during the meeting, the learner can obtain some facts and authoritative opinions that should aid him to participate in a meaningful way. Reading this digest of various aspects of the topic is not a substitute for well-rounded study, but it is better than no preparation at all. Sometimes briefs are the only feasible way to promote advance preparation by the participants.

Example:

A group of agencies are cooperating in an educational program for adults. The purpose of the program is to improve the eating habits of the families in a particular neighborhood. The program consists of the various kinds of activities including large group meetings held in schools and churches. One meeting is devoted to the topic "Eating Better Breakfasts." After seeing a film and hearing facts presented by an expert, by means of an interview, the 60 persons in the audience are divided into four discussion groups. Each group, with a trained leader and a resource person, is to discuss the topic "What Do We Have To Gain by Eating Better Breakfasts?" The planning committee decides to distribute an information brief to the discussion groups for these reasons:

1. It will summarize the facts brought out earlier in the evening by means of the film and the interview;
2. Reading it should give some persons the confidence they need to participate in the discussion;
3. Providing the learner with something tangible to take home (and to show to other persons) increases the chances that he will take steps to improve his eating habits.

Since the audience is made up of persons of widely different educational levels, the committee makes sure that the information brief is written in simple language. They also should guard against developing an information brief that has the effect of stopping discussion rather than stimulating it. So they make certain that the brief does not answer all the questions that may be raised by the discussion topic.

At the meeting, each leader will allow time for his group members to look over the information brief before he starts the discussion. In some instances, the leader may read the brief aloud in order to promote understanding of it and to focus the attention of the group participants.

B. *Who prepares the information brief?*

1. A member or members of the planning committee can accept this responsibility;

2. Someone in the learning group itself (those who will be at the meeting) can be requested to prepare a brief with guidance from a member of the planning committee;

3. A resource person can be requested to furnish one;

4. Information briefs can be prepared by staff members of public, college, school, or special libraries;

5. Some colleges and universities have special agencies that assist people with tasks of this kind.

C. *Some suggestions*

1. Do not try to include a great deal of information—only major points, issues, facts, and opinions;

2. Give the source of all direct quotations that are used—i.e., the author, title, publisher, date of publication, and page number;

3. Try to present an objective, well-rounded point of view. On controversial issues, give various sides and opinions;

4. If the information brief is designed to promote discussion, guard against including information that will tend to discourage discussion;

5. Use language that the reader can understand;

6. List some references for further study;

7. Do not rely on the information brief as a substitute for more thorough preparation and follow-up study.

D. *A sample information brief*

This brief has been used successfully in many learning groups.

COMMUNITY AGENCIES WORK
WITH OLDER ADULTS

The number of people over 65 has tripled since 1900. The average American has gained 19 years of life in the last 50 years. Many communities already have larger numbers of older adults in their population than ever before. Community agencies have a two-fold role in relation to these groups of older adults. One part of this role is to help men and women of all ages prepare for older age and for retirement. The other part of the role is to find the best ways to use the skills and experiences of these men and women as resources in all kinds of community activity.

WHAT ARE THE RESPONSIBILITIES OF COMMUNITY
AGENCIES IN RELATION TO THE AGING?

1. Serving as source of information on all aspects of the aging process;

2. Making people aware that material on the aging process is available;

3. Considering the needs of the aged person as an individual (selection of materials and referrals to other agencies):

    a. Plans for retirement;

    b. Information for the volunteer who helps with the community activities for aging;

    c. Books with large print;

    d. Referrals to services to the blind;

    e. Material for the professional worker who serves the aging, social workers, ministers, superintendents of nursing homes, community recreation leaders, librarians;

4. Providing group services to the aging;

    a. Through cooperation with other agencies providing such services;

    b. Through library-sponsored book reviews, discussion groups, local history groups, hobby clubs, etc.

For Discussion

1. How can we help the community identify the needs of the aging?

2. Advantages and disadvantages of starting a committee on aging in our community;

3. Other courses of action open to us.

Suggested Reading

Blackshear, Orrilla. *Public Library Serves the Aging*. Wisconsin Library Bulletin, Vol. 52, No. 2, March-April, 1956 (may be borrowed from ALA Headquarters Library);

Package Library Briefs. *Opportunities for the Aging*. Vol. 13, No. 1, September, 1956. Available from Indiana University, Bureau of Public Discussion, Bloomington, Indiana, 35¢;

Selected References on Aging, an annotated bibliography. 1955. Compiled for the Committee on Aging by the Library of the U.S. Department of Health, Education, and Welfare. For sale by the Superintendent of Documents, U.S. Government Printing Office, Washington 25, D.C., 30¢.

CHAPTER 6

Designing and Conducting Clinics, Institutes, and Workshops

I. Distinguishing between the Clinic, Institute, and Workshop

Adults can learn systematically over an extended period of time by means of three basic types of meetings: the clinic, the institute, and the workshop. These meetings usually extend from one day to several weeks or longer. They may involve from 25 to 300 or more people. While the three basic types have some features in common, there are differences in emphases that can be summed up as follows:

A. Clinic

The clinic places emphasis on diagnosing and analyzing problems and seeking solutions to them. The approach is through situations designed to reveal existing conditions (in an organization, institution, community, etc.). Case studies, demonstrations, role-playing, speeches, and field trips are the most frequently used techniques. The group confronts life-like situations in order to learn to meet them more successfully.

B. Institute

Authoritative instruction is emphasized. An organized body of knowledge is presented to the learners—or issues are raised for their consideration. Training in a skill may also be offered. Educational techniques and aids frequently used are: the speech, symposium, interview, panel, colloquy, forum, films, and exhibits. The participants learn in groups but individual study is also encouraged.

C. Workshop

The workshop allows considerable flexibility. Emphasis is on improving individual proficiency and understanding. Theory and practice are often treated concurrently. The learner is encouraged to work out a program of personal study, for which he receives help from other participants and resource people. The learning situations tend to be based on interests and needs identified by the participants themselves (rather than by experts).

Clinics, institutes, and workshops usually involve both *general sessions,* during which the entire group meets together, and *subgroup meetings* of the following types:

1. *Special interest groups* offer opportunities for 15 to 50 persons with similar concerns and background to learn under the guidance of resource persons. Information is presented in these sessions similarly as it is done in the general sessions, since they are not primarily designed for audience participation. An important point to remember is that persons of similar concerns and background should be assigned to the same group. Often a person comes to an institute with his employer, supervisor, or a person with more status or experience. In this case, it may be wise to assign these persons to different groups. Other factors to take into account in assigning a person to a specific group are: the preferences of the person himself, his age, sex, occupation, and the extent of his knowledge of the topic.

2. *Work groups* are composed of 10 to 25 participants who have been assigned on the basis of personal interest or experience, profession, or vocation. In each meeting, work is done on problems, projects, or other assignments. Whether or not the work group reports its accomplishments to the other participants will depend on its purpose.

3. *Discussion groups.* Groups of 10 to 20 persons who converse about issues or discussable topics under the guidance of a trained discussion leader. The group may develop its own agenda or have its agenda determined in advance by those responsible for planning.

4. *Practice groups.* 10 to 15 persons meet for opportunities to practice a skill under expert guidance. For example, if a workshop

dealt with "Parliamentary Procedure," practice groups might offer each participant a chance to run a business meeting.

A clinic, institute, or workshop usually has a *coordinator*. His job is to offer leadership and guidance throughout the planning and conducting of the meeting. He assumes final responsibility for such tasks as setting up committees, orientation of resource people and leaders, and liaison with the parent organizations or sponsors.

In addition, there is usually the *staff*, which conducts the workshop, clinic, or institute. The staff may act alternately as instructors, discussion leaders, or resource persons. The staff may or may not be the same persons who have done the planning.

In addition to the staff there may be *resource persons* who present information and authoritative opinion in the general sessions and in the subgroup meetings. They sometimes make systematic presentations through techniques like the speech, symposium, or the demonstration. In the discussion groups, their role is that of supplying information upon the request of the leaders and participants. If practice groups are held, the resource persons show the participants how to carry out procedures and offer opportunities for the participants to practice the use of these procedures.

II. Examples of Clinics, Institutes, and Workshops

A. *Three clinics*

1. A group of local membership chairmen for an organization meet to examine and try to solve the problem of a decreasing membership. Under the guidance of a consultant from their national headquarters, they plan a clinic designed to (1) analyze existing policies about membership and recruitment, (2) share ideas relating to their problem, and (3) analyze the cases of one of their local organizations with a good record in getting new members and one with a poor record.

2. A group of local churches are having difficulties using a fund-raising system developed by their denominational headquarters. District church leaders hold a clinic designed to assist

the leaders from the local churches to overcome their problems and to examine the results in one or two churches using the fund-raising system. The learning experience is under the guidance of several local leaders who have had a great deal of experience with the fund-raising system and of one of their denomination's fund-raising specialists from national headquarters.

3. The training department in a boat company has a request to assist the company's salesmen to become more effective in the selling of sailboats. About 50 salesmen are involved. One salesman with an especially good sales record is available to act as a resource person. The training department, which has six members, becomes the staff for a clinic to be held on the problem "How Can We Sell More Sailboats?"

It becomes clear that two kinds of sessions will be needed: (1) demonstration of selling procedures carried out by the resource person, and one or more persons taking the role of the customer; and (2) discussion groups in which the participants attempt to discover and explore new approaches to the problem of increasing sales. After going further into the planning, the clinic staff discovers that the participants do not have adequate knowledge of the product they are trying to sell. So it becomes clear that the clinic should include a field trip to the company's sailboat plant and some firsthand experience in sailing. The clinic is therefore held at an appropriate location which has facilities adequate to demonstrate a variety of sales tactics.

The final program might look like this:

SALES CLINIC

Theme: *How Can We Sell More Sailboats?*
Goals: To demonstrate tested approaches to selling sailboats,
           To learn more about the product we are selling,
           To discuss ways to encourage sales.

Schedule

Monday
9:00-10:00 a.m.   Registration, Orientation, Getting Acquainted
10:00-12:00 Noon Field trip to the plant
2:00- 5:00 p.m.   Demonstrations and opportunities to operate sailboats

226

8:00- 9:00 p.m.	Discussion Groups—"What Do Our Experiences Today Suggest for Better Selling?" (Three groups of about 15 persons each—all groups discuss the same topic.)
Tuesday	
9:00-10:00 a.m.	Panel—"Some Suggestions for Improving Sales" (The leaders of the three discussion groups held the previous evening discuss the various ideas brought out under the guidance of a moderator from the clinic staff.)
10:00-11:30 a.m.	Demonstrations of selling procedures (conducted by the resource person and the clinic staff)
11:30-12:00 Noon	Summary and Conclusions (speech by the resource person)
12:00-12:30 p.m.	Evaluation and Written Recommendations (sent to the training staff and the production department and used to improve future meetings).

B. Three institutes

1. An institute for group discussion leaders and participants (to teach people how to carry on effective group discussion): these institutes provide from 6 to 12 hours of planned and supervised instruction and practice for about 30 persons. The institute is designed and conducted by persons who are specialists in the information and skills to be taught. At general sessions, information is presented to the total group by means of speeches, films, and demonstrations. During the greater part of the time, the total group is divided into two practice groups, each guided by a trainer or instructor. In these smaller groups, the institute members take part in supervised practice discussions which enable them to gain first-hand experience in properly leading and participating in group discussion.

2. An institute on "New Approaches to Patient Care" was held for nursing personnel from several hospitals. It was planned and conducted by college faculty members in a school of nursing together with experienced registered nurses. An investigator who

had been developing experimental patient care programs in hospitals served as resource person. The purposes of the meeting were to provide specific instruction about new concepts and practices.

The participants took part in general sessions, practice sessions, and discussion groups. In the general sessions, they learned about new concepts and practices in caring for patients. In the practice sessions, they tried out some of these practices. And in the discussion groups they explored ways of putting new concepts and practices into effect in their back-home situations.

The program looked like this:

INSTITUTE

Theme: *New Approaches to Patient Care*
Goals: To offer practical instruction in new approaches to patient care,
To provide practice opportunities for all participants,
To promote better patient care,
To make available the findings of recent research.
Sponsors: State Nurses Association and Community Hospital

Schedule

9:00- 9:15 a.m.	"Welcome and Orientation"
9:15-10:05 a.m.	"Three New Approaches" Symposium-Forum
10:30-12:00 Noon	Practice Sessions (Participants meet in small groups to try out new approaches to patient care)
1:30- 2:45 p.m.	Discussion Groups—"How Can We Apply What We Have Learned?"
3:00- 4:30 p.m.	Reports from Discussion Groups, Evaluation, and Closing Remarks.

3. Chapter Two contains a complete example of the planning of an institute in a local parent-teacher association.

C. A workshop

Some adults in an urban community are interested in providing better summer recreation opportunities for their children. Parents of five families that are especially concerned begin meeting to discuss the problem. They invite a professional recreation worker to meet with them. In consultation with their neighbors, this group begins to organize a learning experience that will help the participating families to learn about summer recreation activities available to them.

The committee decides to hold a workshop for these reasons:

1. The adults who will participate in the learning experience have somewhat different needs, depending on the size of the family, type of home facilities available, and the ages of their children—considerable flexibility, therefore, is required;

2. Each family should be able to work out plans for family recreation.

The workshop will be held at an elementary school in order to have playground facilities and numerous rooms available. Resource persons for the workshop will be drawn from city recreation personnel. At the general sessions, the resource persons will present information about recreation to the adults. Then in the practice sessions, the children will join their parents for opportunities to learn new recreational activities. The program will look like this:

FAMILY RECREATION WORKSHOP

Theme: *Family Recreation This Summer*

Goals: To discover recreation facilities now available,
To learn how to use present facilities,
To learn how to assume responsibility for, and to conduct, a portion of their family recreational programs.

Date: Saturday, May 25th

Place: North Side School

General Session

9:00- 9:10 a.m.	"The Nature and Purpose of This Workshop" (Speech by workshop coordinator)
9:10- 9:30 a.m.	"Some Suggestions About Family Recreation" (Neighborhood recreation director interviewed by a parent)
9:30-10:00 a.m.	"Outdoor Games for Families" (film)

Practice Groups

10:00-12:00 a.m.   Group 1—Badminton
                    Group 2—Croquet
                    Group 3—Volley ball
                    Group 4—Nature study
                    Group 5—Camping
                    Group 6—Indoor activities

General Session

1:30- 3:00 p.m.   "Overcoming Obstacles to Family Recreation"

Work Groups

3:00- 4:30 p.m.   (Each family works out a plan for family recreation and gets the reaction of a resource person and of other participants)

III. DECISIONS DURING PLANNING

(In Chapter Two of this book, there is a detailed account of the planning of an institute.)

Among the many decisions that must be made during the planning of a clinic, institute, or workshop, the following are essential.

A. *Goals and evaluation*

What is to be accomplished? What problems are to be dealt with, information presented, or changes brought about? Why is a group learning experience advisable? What plans for evaluation are to be made?

B. *Participation*

Who should be involved? Who can profit from the experience? What is the audience for whom the learning situation is to be designed? Should participation be limited and if so, how?

C. *General type of meeting*

Will a clinic, or an institute, or a workshop be most appropriate?

D. Physical location and arrangements

Where will the meeting be held? What meeting rooms, dining and sleeping facilities will be required?

E. Budget

What will the costs be? How will the meeting be financed? How much will each participant be assessed?

F. Promotion and publicity

How will promotion and publicity be handled? What features will be emphasized? How can the participants' interest and active involvement be initiated and sustained?

G. Leadership and resources

Who will act as coordinator, staff, and resource people? What persons will be needed for leadership roles such as panel moderators and chairmen for the general sessions?

H. Design of specific sessions

Each session in the total program should be designed to be an effective learning situation. This involves the proper use of techniques, subtechniques, and educational aids (see Chapters Three, Four, and Five).

I. Registration and orientation

Will there be advance registration? How will registration be handled? What advance orientation will the participants receive? How will advance study or preparation be encouraged?

J. Committees

What committees will be organized? Frequently committees are established to deal with most of the items previously noted in this list; i.e., a committee for evaluation, promotion, program design.

231

IV. A Check List for Planning

	Yes	No	Unde-cided
1. Do we have clear-cut goals to achieve?	___	___	___
2. Have we carefully decided on the type of meeting to be held (that is workshop, institute, or clinic)?	___	___	___
3. Can adequate facilities be provided for:			
a. The general sessions?	___	___	___
b. The small group meetings?	___	___	___
4. Do we have the necessary:			
a. Study materials?	___	___	___
b. Equipment (for example, film projector if one is to be used)?	___	___	___
c. Funds?	___	___	___
5. Is our theme of interest to those expected to participate in the institute?	___	___	___
6. Is there definitely a need for:			
a. Special interest groups?	___	___	___
b. Practice groups?	___	___	___
c. Discussion groups?	___	___	___
d. Work groups?	___	___	___
7. If discussion groups are to be held, can each be led by a trained leader?	___	___	___
8. Do we have available as resource persons, people who:			
a. Know their subject thoroughly?	___	___	___
b. Know how to instruct adults?	___	___	___
c. Know how to participate as a resource person?	___	___	___
d. Will communicate interest and enthusiasm?	___	___	___
e. Will remain available for consultation with individual participants?	___	___	___

9. Have we selected the proper techniques, subtechniques, and educational aids for each meeting? _____ _____ _____

10. Do we have available a competent coordinator? _____ _____ _____

11. Is there evidence that the expected participants:

a. Are interested in the topic or procedures that will be treated? _____ _____ _____

b. Are capable of learning what is to be taught? _____ _____ _____

c. Are willing to take the time to attend? _____ _____ _____

12. Do we have sound plans for:

a. Promotion? _____ _____ _____

b. Publicity? _____ _____ _____

13. Have we provided for:

a. Advance study? _____ _____ _____

b. Orientation prior to arrival? _____ _____ _____

14. Do we have a printed program that:

a. Stimulates interest? _____ _____ _____

b. Clarifies our goals? _____ _____ _____

15. Have we provided for evaluation? _____ _____ _____

16. Have we provided for follow-up study? _____ _____ _____

17. Have we provided for briefing of the:

a. Discussion leaders? _____ _____ _____

b. Chairmen of each session? _____ _____ _____

c. Resource persons? _____ _____ _____

d. Other persons with special responsibilities (e.g., panel moderators, role-players, interviewer)? _____ _____ _____

18. Have we provided for:

a. Hospitality? _____ _____ _____

b. Recreation? _____ _____ _____

V. A CHECK LIST FOR EVALUATION

This check list is for the use of (a) the coordinator and the staff and (b) those who take part in the meeting.

If the trend of replies to the questions is toward "no" and "undecided," the clinic, institute, or workshop probably has been conducted ineffectively; future errors can be avoided if the various replies are discussed by the coordinator and the staff.

	Yes	No	Unde-cided
1. Was the promotion effective?	___	___	___
2. Did the participants understand what was expected of them?	___	___	___
3. Were the meeting facilities adequate?	___	___	___
4. Were the dining and housing facilities adequate?	___	___	___
5. Was registration handled effectively?	___	___	___
6. Were helpful study materials made available?	___	___	___
7. Were the general sessions:			
a. Relatively free from distractions?	___	___	___
b. Characterized by good physical arrangements?	___	___	___
c. Made meaningful by clear presentation?	___	___	___
d. Appropriate in length and number?	___	___	___
e. Clear as to goals and purposes?	___	___	___
f. Effective as to the use made of educational techniques, subtechniques, and aids?	___	___	___
8. Were the special interest groups (if used):			
a. Made up of persons who:			
(1) Had common interests?	___	___	___
(2) Could work together?	___	___	___
(3) Were similar in background?	___	___	___
b. Adequate as to physical arrangements?	___	___	___
c. Well conducted?	___	___	___

234

d. Staffed with the appropriate resource persons?

e. Clear as to their goals and task? ___ ___ ___

f. Appropriate as to:

(1) Frequency of meeting? ___ ___ ___

(2) Length? ___ ___ ___

g. Effective as to the use made of educational techniques, subtechniques, and aids? ___ ___ ___

9. Were the discussion, practice, or work groups (if used):

a. Well conducted? ___ ___ ___

b. In suitable surroundings? ___ ___ ___

c. Clear as to their:

(1) Task? ___ ___ ___

(2) Responsibilities to the total group? ___ ___ ___

d. Appropriate as to:

(1) Length? ___ ___ ___

(2) Frequency of meeting? ___ ___ ___

10. Did the coordinator and staff:

a. Carry out responsibilities? ___ ___ ___

b. See that the group was well oriented:

(1) Prior to arrival? ___ ___ ___

(2) After arrival? ___ ___ ___

c. See that schedules were met? ___ ___ ___

d. Properly instruct the resource persons? ___ ___ ___

e. Help the participants to learn? ___ ___ ___

f. Remain flexible and able to make adjustments to aid learning? ___ ___ ___

11. Did the resource people? ___ ___ ___

a. Understand their responsibilities? ___ ___ ___

b. Understand the techniques they were involved in? ___ ___ ___

c. Use understandable language? ___ ___ ___

d. Use helpful examples? ___ ___ ___

e. Remain available for consultation? ___ ___ ___

f. Present information clearly and effectively? ___ ___ ___

12. Did the participants:

a. Make advance preparation? _____ _____ _____

b. Make use of their opportunities for learning? _____ _____ _____

c. Attend meetings on time? _____ _____ _____

d. Cooperate with the coordinator and the resource persons? _____ _____ _____

13. What was accomplished: _____ _____ _____

a. Was useful information presented in the general sessions? _____ _____ _____

b. Did the participants show evidence of having acquired information, new viewpoints, or of having changed attitudes? _____ _____ _____

c. Was progress made toward the goals? _____ _____ _____

d. Have problems or needs emerged which point toward further study or action? _____ _____ _____

e. Was there evidence of willingness to accept responsibility for further study or action? _____ _____ _____

Appendix

An Annotated Reading List Concerning Adult Education Procedures

This list of suggested readings contains books and pamphlets. Articles in magazines and journals are not included.

PROCEDURES IN ADULT EDUCATION

1. Beckhard, Richard. *How to Plan and Conduct Workshops and Conferences.* New York: Association Press, 1956, 64 pp.

    In addition to the steps in planning large group meetings, this book includes suggestions for setting up special interest groups, and for handling registration and evaluation.

2. Bergevin, Paul and McKinley, John. *Design for Adult Education in the Church.* New York: The Seabury Press, 1961, 320 pp.

    This book contains an idea for effectively training adults to assume responsibilities for planning and carrying out adult learning activities. Along with this idea it treats adult education techniques, leadership and participation in learning groups, conditions for effective adult learning, and ways of determining needs and interests of adults.

3. Bergevin, Paul and Morris, Dwight. *Group Processes for Adult Education.* New York: The Seabury Press, 1960, 86 pp.

    A useful booklet for those interested in broadening their knowledge about techniques used in adult education activities. The following are treated in outline form: speech, speech-forum, panel, panel-forum, symposium (modern concept), symposium-forum (modern concept), symposium (ancient concept), colloquy, group discussion, conference, convention, committee, institute, seminar, and workship.

4. Bergevin, Paul and Morris, Dwight. *A Manual for Group Discussion Participants.* New York: The Seabury Press, 1965, 64 pp.

    An easy-to-use manual for those interested in knowing more about group discussion.

5. Cartwright, Dorwin and Zander, Alvin. *Group Dynamics: Research and Theory*. New York: Harper and Row, 3rd ed., 1968.

   A comprehensive summary of theory and research in group dynamics. Material is grouped in categories with interpretive chapters introducing each category.

6. Kelley, Earl C. *The Workshop Way of Learning*. New York: Harper and Brothers, 1951, 169 pp.

   This book discusses in detail the workshop learning experience as the author used it for teacher-training and lay groups, to solve problems cooperatively. The stress is on teacher training. The author discusses both the long and short workshop.

7. Klein, Alan F. *Role Playing*. New York: Association Press, 1956, 176 pp.

   This book discusses in detail the characteristics of role-playing and how to use role-playing for educational purposes. It includes numerous examples.

8. Knowles, Malcolm and Hulda. *Introduction to Group Dynamics*. New York: Association Press, 1959, 87 pp.

   Described by the author as "not a how to do" but a "how to find out book," this brief work is a guide and a preparation for further study of the findings of social scientists investigating the characteristics of groups.

9. Lasker, Bruno. *Democracy Through Discussion*. New York: H. W. Wilson Company, 1949, 376 pp.

   Mr. Lasker goes into the "why" of learning in small groups. He measures group discussion against a yardstick of "democracy as a way of life."

10. Powell, John Walker. *Education for Maturity*. New York: Hermitage House, 1949, 242 pp.

    The author outlines the stages that learning groups pass through, and discusses some unique characteristics of adult discussion groups.

11. Wilson, Meredith and Gallup, Gladys. *Extension Teaching Methods*. Extension Service Circular 495, August, 1955. U.S. Department of Agriculture, Washington, D.C., 80 pp.

    This brochure explains what workers in the field of Agricultural Extension have learned about using certain procedures to influence rural families to adopt agricultural and home economics practices.

12. Zelko, Harold P. *Successful Conference and Discussion Techniques*. New York: McGraw-Hill, 1957, 264 pp.

    This book emphasizes group discussion fundamentals. It contains aids for program planning and discussion leadership.

LEADERSHIP

1. Frank, Lawrence K. *How To Be a Modern Leader*. New York: Association Press, Leadership Library Series, 1954, 62 pp.
   A general discussion of what is involved in group leadership together with a philosophy of leadership.
2. Gordon, Thomas. *Group-Centered Leadership*. New York: Houghton Mifflin, 1955, 366 pp.
   The author develops and illustrates the concept that the best source of leadership ultimately is the group members themselves, rather than persons designated or chosen as leaders.
3. *Leadership Library Series*. New York: Association Press.
   A series of short books treating leadership, committee work, planning workshops, and the uses of audio-visual aids.
4. *Leadership Pamphlets*. Adult Education Association of the U.S.A., 743 North Wabash Avenue, Chicago 11, Illinois.
   A series of pamphlets treating the problems of working with volunteers, planning programs, conducting workshops, getting and keeping members, and taking community action.
5. Liveright, A. A. *Strategies of Leadership*. New York: Harper and Brothers, 1959, 135 pp.
   Written for volunteer and professional leaders, this book contains suggestions for analyzing adult education programs in terms of their leadership responsibilities.
6. Ross, Murray G. and Hendry, Charles. *New Understandings of Leadership*. New York: Association Press, 1957, 158 pp.
   The authors summarize recent research and thought about the nature and meaning of leadership. Included are theory, research findings, and a suggested program for developing leaders in business, social, and educational organizations.
7. Thelen, Herbert A. *Dynamics of Groups at Work*. Chicago: University of Chicago Press, 1954. 379 pp.
   This book discusses many aspects of group behavior. Its insights seem most useful for consultants, trainers, and other professional adult education workers.
8. Trecker, Audrey and Harleigh. *How To Work With Groups*. New York: Woman's Press, 1952, 167 pp.
   The authors treat such volunteer leadership responsibilities as P.T.A. presidents and committee chairmen, group discussion, finance, and publicity. A section on how to deal with the conflicts in an adult group is included.

A Glossary of Terms Relating to Adult Education Procedures

Acceptance. A positive and uncensuring attitude toward a person; recognition of his worth as a person without condemning or condoning his actions or expressions.

Adult. A person who has reached physical maturity.

Adult Education. The process through which adults have and use opportunities to learn systematically under the guidance of an agency, teacher, or leader; experiences in day-to-day living which cause adult behavioral change; the study of the professional field of adult education.

In a free society a kind of education which promotes a mature rationality in our adult lives and institutions.

Agenda. Something to be done; items of business to be brought before a meeting or topics to be discussed.

Aids, Educational. Resources such as pamphlets, exhibits, annotated bibliographies, case histories, audio-visual materials and information briefs, which assist in the learning process through the employment of the several senses.

Aim. A foreseen end that can be used to give direction to an activity or to motivate behavior.

Annotated Bibliography or Reading List. A list of readings with notes to indicate the nature of the content treated and in some instances to give an evaluation of the content.

Appraisal. An estimation of the effectiveness of an adult education procedure.

Attitude. A state of mental and emotional readiness to react to situations, persons, or things in a manner in harmony with an habitual pattern of response.

Audience Reaction Team. A group of three to five audience representatives who interrupt a speaker or other resource person at appropriate times to seek immediate clarification on points that seem obscure, or to assist the speaker to treat the needs of the persons present.

Authoritarian. A person who advocates the principle of obedience to authority as opposed to individual liberty or self-direction.

Authority. An accepted source of information, direction, or guidance.

Autocrat. A person who exercises absolute power or unlimited authority.

240

Behavior. Action or activity which a person manifests in reacting to ideas, things, or people.

Buzz Session. An audience divided into several small (buzz) groups, meeting simultaneously, to discuss a topic assigned them or perform a task.

Case History. An educational aid consisting of a written description of an event, incident, or situation. Used by learners as resource material to analyze and discuss.

Chairman. The person who is normally in charge of an educational meeting—opening and closing it and providing the necessary transition from one part to the next.

Clinic. An extended series of meetings that involves diagnosis, analysis, and treatment of conditions or problems.

Colloquy. A modification of the panel using six or eight persons— three or four representing the audience and three or four resource persons. The colloquy members, selected from and representing the audience, ask questions, express opinions, and raise issues to be treated by the resource persons.

Co-Leader. In group discussion, if two persons share leadership, they are called co-leaders.

Committee. A small group of persons appointed or elected to perform a task that cannot be done efficiently by an entire group or organization, or done effectively by one person.

Communication. A process by which people influence one another by transmitting and receiving ideas, opinions, feelings, and attitudes.

Communication, Pattern of. A systematic arrangement which defines the origin, direction, and end of the flow of verbal participation by the members of a learning group.

Community. A society of people having common rights and privileges, or common interests, civil, political, or ecclesiastical, usually living in one locality under the same culture. Can be any group of people, not necessarily in spatial proximity, who share basic interests and traditions.

Content. Mainly the substantive information (subject matter) in a learning program. The "what" of education as compared with the "how." The "what" could be considered content, the "how" process. In program planning, the topics developed for treatment in the learning activity being planned.

Convention. An assembly of members, representatives, or delegates from local units of a parent organization meeting together for the purpose of transacting business, sharing experiences, solving problems, and gaining information.

Criterion. A standard of judgment accepted as a basis for comparison or evaluation.

Critique. A portion of a meeting in which the participants analyze (as objectively as possible) the strengths and weaknesses of their educational activity.

Demonstration. A carefully prepared presentation that shows how to perform an act or use a procedure.

Educational Aid. See *Aids.*

Exhibit. A collection of related items displayed to aid learning.

Evaluation. Judging the effectiveness of an adult education experience in terms of the goals.

Field Trip. A planned educational tour in which a group visits an object or place of interest for first-hand observation and study.

Forum. A 15- to 60-minute period of open discussion that is carried on among the members of an entire group and one or more resource persons.

Goal. The objective or end toward which a learning experience is directed, the expected results; a specific statement of intention to meet a need.

Group Discussion. A purposeful conversation and deliberation about a topic of mutual interest among 6 to 20 participants under the guidance of a trained participant called a leader.

Group Dynamics. Sociological and psychological forces at work in any group situation. Also, the scientific study of these forces.

Group Participant. A member of a learning team who takes an active part in the educational process as one of the learners in the group.

Group Process. The factors which are concerned with *how* persons learn together (the way) as contrasted to *what* they learn (the content).

Idea Inventory. Sometimes called "brainstorming" or "freewheeling," is the spontaneous outpouring of ideas pertinent to an area of interest or need about which a group desires to reach a decision.

Information Brief. An educational aid consisting of one to three pages of specific information about a topic. The brief is distributed to participants in advance of or during the educational meeting where the topic will be treated.

Institute. An extended series of meetings which provide specific and authoritative instruction by qualified specialists.

Institution. An established pattern of social or cultural traits which has a degree of permanence even though the persons within it may change.

Interest. Something a learner would like to learn about or come to understand better. Used as a basis to identify needs which can be treated educationally.

Interview. A 5 to 30 minute presentation conducted before an audience in which one or two resource persons respond to systematic questioning by an interviewer about a previously determined topic.

Issue. A presentation of alternatives between which the persons in a group may choose or decide.

Leader. Any member of a learning team who accepts the responsibilities of leading the other participants in adult educational endeavors.

Listening and Observing Groups. An audience divided into two or three groups each of which is assigned the task of listening and observing a certain part of a speech, demonstration, panel, etc.

Maturity. A condition of highest development in the areas of human psychological, moral, sexual, social, and spiritual relationships. Characterized as a process of becoming rather than being.

Method. An established or systematic order for performing any act or conducting any operation. The relationship established by an educational institution with a group of participants for the purpose of systematically diffusing knowledge among them. Some methods of adult education are correspondence study, the coordinated course, and community development.

Moderator. A person who introduces and guides discussion and audience participation during a panel, colloquy, or forum.

Need (Educational). A lack or deficiency which may be satisfied by means of a learning experience.

Need (Felt). Something regarded as necessary by the person concerned.

Need (Real Educational). What a person lacks and which might be acquired through learning. Based on an accepted standard of values.

Need (Symptomatic Educational). A manifestation of a need which a person considers real; could be used as a clue to a real need.

Objective. A specific end or goal that learners are trying to reach. Usually refers to a readily attainable end or goal.

Observer. A trained person in an educational program who objectively watches and listens to the forces at work in a learning group.

Panel. The panel is a group of three to six persons having a purposeful conversation of an assigned topic. The panel is usually seated at a table in full view of an audience.

Participant. A person trained as a member of a learning team. All of the members of the learning group are participants assuming different roles: group participants, leaders, resource persons, and observers.

Participant, Group. See *Group Participant.*

Participation. The sharing of a variety of responsibilities in an educational venture.

Problem, Educational. A condition or obstacle that learners seek to overcome through the use of various problem-solving procedures.

Procedure. A systematic series of steps designed to accomplish a task.

Process. The procedural intra- and inter-personal factors involved in how a person learns in contrast to what he learns (content).

Program. An educational meeting or series of meetings based on the interests and needs of the expected participants. Such an event is usually planned to achieve certain educational goals.

Program, Printed. A printed description of an educational meeting or series of meetings.

Program Planning. A procedure by which the nature and sequence of future educational programs are determined.

Purposes. The immediate tasks that will be performed in an educational program; differs slightly from "goal" and "objective" in that goals and objectives often refer to ultimate outcomes. Purposes are sometimes called declarations of intent.

Question Period. A 5 to 20 minute portion of a meeting during which audience members ask questions of a speaker or other resource person.

Quiet Meeting. A 15 to 60 minute period of meditation and limited verbal expression by a group of five or more persons. This technique is characterized by periods of silence and by occasional spontaneous verbal contributions by members of the group.

Recorder. A participant who accepts the responsibility to write down the salient points that emerge during the course of an adult learning experience. The participants can make use of this information for summarizing and keeping a permanent record.

Resources. Educational materials or aids from which persons in an educational situation may seek information. The adult educator uses such resources as audio-visual materials, printed matter, charts, graphs, and maps.

Resource Person. An expert or authority who contributes information and opinion to participants in a learning situation.

Role-Playing. A spontaneous portrayal (acting out) of a situation, condition, or circumstance by selected members of a learning group.

244

Screening Panel. A group of three to five representative members of an audience who discuss with each other the educational needs of the audience they represent in order to reveal this information to a speaker or resource person. The discussion is carried on in the presence of the audience.

Seminar. A technique involving 5 to 30 persons led in systematic study by a recognized authority in the subject being studied.

Skill. Anything that a person has learned to do with ease and precision; may be either a physical or mental performance.

Speech. A carefully prepared oral presentation of a subject by a qualified person; also known as a lecture.

Subject. A division or field of organized knowledge to be treated during a learning experience.

Subtechnique. An educational instrument employed to modify and enhance the effectiveness of a technique.

Symposium (Ancient). A group of 5 to 20 persons meet in a home or private dining room to enjoy good food, entertainment, fellowship, and discussion of a topic of mutual interest.

Symposium (Modern). A series of related speeches by two to five persons qualified to speak with authority on different phases of the same topic or on closely related topics.

Task. A specific job or work assignment; a defined mission.

Technique. The way in which the adult educator arranges the relationships of learners and resources to assist the learners to acquire knowledge in a learning situation.

Theme. The general, descriptive title used to describe the nature of a meeting or series of meetings; the main subject to be treated.

Topic(s). In group discussion the main subject, problem, or issue to be discussed. In program planning, defines the desired information—the problems, issues, questions, and concepts—which the program will treat (i.e., the topics represent the potential content of the program).

Trainer. An adult educator (professional or lay) who uses recognized adult education procedures and teaches others to use them.

Workshop. A type of meeting that offers opportunities for persons with a common interest or problem to meet with specialists to receive firsthand knowledge and practice.